25 Complex Text Passages to Meet the Common Core

Literature and Informational Texts

Grade 5

by Martin Lee and Marcia Miller

Jumping Up Learning Circles
5965 Almaden Expressway #165
San Jose, CA 95120
408-323-8388

NEW YORK ● TORONTO ● LONDON ● AUCKLAND ● SYDNEY
MEXICO CITY ● NEW DELHI ● HONG KONG ● BUENOS AIRES

Teaching
Resources

Editor: Mela Ottaiano
Cover design: Scott Davis
Interior design: Kathy Massaro

Interior illustrations: O&A Ivanov (pages 26, 28, and 34); Margeaux Lucas (page 30); Hector Borlasca (page 36); Teresa Anderko (pages 38, 42, and 68). Illustrations copyright © 2014 by Scholastic Inc.

Image credits: page 32 © klosfoto/iStockphoto; page 44 © anacarol/Shutterstock, Inc.; page 46 © North Wind Picture Archives/Alamy; page 48 © Denis Farrell/AP; page 52 © North Wind Picture Archives/Alamy; page 56 © Bayanova Svetlana/Shutterstock, Inc.; page 60 © Everett Collection/SuperStock; page 62 © Brian_Brockman/iStockphoto; page 64 © De Agostini/Getty Images; page 66 © sshepard/iStockphoto; page 70 © Jorge Saenz/AP; page 72 © photka/Shutterstock, Inc.; page 74 © Alfredo Caliz/Panos.

ISBN: 978-0-545-57711-3
Copyright © 2014 by Scholastic Inc.
All rights reserved.
Printed in the U.S.A.
Published by Scholastic Inc.

1 2 3 4 5 6 7 8 9 10   40   21 20 19 18 17 16 15 14

Contents

> "To build a foundation for college and career readiness, students must read widely and deeply from among a broad range of high-quality, increasingly challenging literary and informational texts. Through extensive reading of stories, dramas, poems, and myths from diverse cultures and different time periods, students gain literary and cultural knowledge as well as familiarity with various text structures and elements. By reading texts in history/social studies, science, and other disciplines, students build a foundation of knowledge in these fields that will also give them the background to be better readers in all content areas. Students can only gain this foundation when the curriculum is intentionally and coherently structured to develop rich content knowledge within and across grades. Students also acquire the habits of reading independently and closely, which are essential to their future success."

—Common Core State Standards for English Language Arts, June 2010

25 Complex Text Passages to Meet the Common Core: Literature and Informational Texts—Grade 5 includes complex reading passages with companion comprehension question pages for teaching the two types of texts—Literature and Informational—covered in the Common Core State Standards (CCSS) for English Language Arts. The passages and lessons in this book address the rigorous expectations put forth by the CCSS "that students read increasingly complex texts through the grades." This book embraces nine of the ten CCSS College and Career Readiness Anchor Standards for Reading that inform solid instruction for literary and informational texts.

Anchor Standards for Reading

Key Ideas and Details

1. Read closely to determine what the text says explicitly and make logical inferences from it; cite specific textual evidence when writing or speaking to support conclusions drawn from the text.

2. Determine central ideas or themes of a text; summarize key supporting details and ideas.

3. Analyze how and why individuals, events, and ideas develop and interact throughout a text.

Craft and Structure

4. Interpret words and phrases as they are used in a text, including determining technical, connotative, and figurative meanings, and analyze how specific word choices shape meaning or tone.

5. Analyze the structure of texts, including how specific sentences, paragraphs, and larger portions of text relate to each other and the whole.

6. Assess how point of view or purpose shapes the content and style of a text.

Integration of Knowledge and Ideas

7. Integrate and evaluate content presented in diverse media and formats, including visually and quantitatively, as well as in words.

8. Delineate and evaluate the argument and specific claims in a text, including the validity of the reasoning as well as the relevance and sufficiency of the evidence.

Range of Reading and Level of Text Complexity

10. Read and comprehend complex literary and informational texts independently and proficiently.

The materials in this book also address the Language Standards, including skills in the conventions of standard English, knowledge of language, and vocabulary acquisition and use. In addition, students meet Writing Standards as they answer questions about the passages, demonstrating their ability to convey ideas coherently, clearly, and with support from the text. On page 12, you'll find a correlation chart that details how the 25 passages meet specific standards. This information can also be found with the teaching notes for each passage on pages 13–25.

About Text Complexity

The CCSS recommend that students tackle increasingly complex texts to develop and hone their skills and knowledge. Many factors contribute to the complexity of any text.

Text complexity is more intricate than a readability score alone reveals. Most formulas examine sentence length and structure and the number of difficult words. Each formula gives different weight to different factors. Other aspects of text complexity include coherence, organization, motivation, and any prior knowledge readers may bring.

A complex text can be relatively easy to decode, but if it examines complex issues or uses figurative language, the overall text complexity rises. By contrast, a text that uses unfamiliar words may be less daunting if readers can apply word-study skills and context clues effectively to determine meaning.

This triangular model used by the CCSS shows three distinct yet interrelated factors that contribute to text complexity.

CCSS Model of Text Complexity

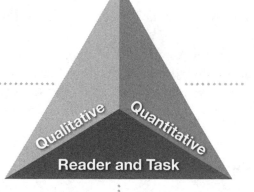

Qualitative measures consider the complexity of meaning or purpose, structure, language conventionality, and overall clarity.

Quantitative measures complexity in terms of word length and frequency, sentence length, and text cohesion. Lexile® algorithms rank this type of complexity on a numerical scale.

Reader and Task considerations refer to such variables as a student's motivation, knowledge, and experience brought to the text, and the purpose, complexity, and types of questions posed.

About the Passages

The 25 reproducible, one-page passages included in this book are divided into two categories. The first 9 passages represent literature (fiction) and are followed by 16 informational texts (nonfiction). Each grouping presents a variety of genres and forms, organizational structures, purposes, tones, and tasks. Consult the table of contents (page 3) to see the scope of genres, forms, and types of content-area texts. The passages within each category are arranged in order of Lexile score (the quantitative measure), from lowest to highest, and fall within the Lexile score ranges recommended for fifth graders. The Lexile scores for grade 5, revised to reflect the more rigorous demands of the CCSS, range from 830 to 1010. For more about determinations of complexity levels, see page 5 and pages 8–9.

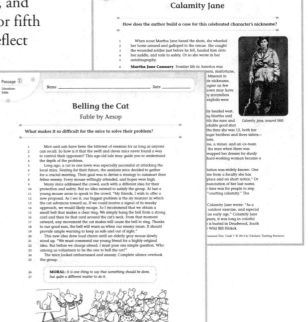

Each passage appears on its own page beginning with the title, the genre or form of the passage, and an opening question to give students a focus to keep in mind as they read. Some passages also include visual elements, such as photographs, drawings, illustrations, or tables, as well as typical text elements, such as italics, boldface type, bulleted or numbered lists, subheadings, or sidebars.

The line numbers that appear to the left of each passage will help you and your students readily locate a specific line of text. For example, students might say, "I'm not sure how to pronounce the name here in line 12." They might also include line numbers to identify text evidence when they answer questions about the piece. For example: "The author says in lines 19–21 that…"

The passages are stand-alone texts, and can be used in any order you choose. Feel free to assign passages to individuals, small groups, or the entire class, as best suits your teaching style. However, it's a good idea to preview each passage before you assign it, to ensure that your students have the skills needed to complete it successfully. (See page 10 for a close-reading routine to model for students.)

About the After-Reading Question Pages

The Common Core standards suggest that assessment should involve "text-dependent questions." Questions constructed to meet this demand guide students to cite evidence from the text. They fall into three broad categories: 1) Key Ideas and Details, 2) Craft and Structure, and 3) Integration of Knowledge and Ideas. According to the standards, responses should include claims supported by the text, connections to informational or literary elements found within the text explicitly or by logical implication, and age-appropriate analyses of themes or topics.

Following each passage is a reproducible page with five text-dependent comprehension questions for students to answer after reading. Two are multiple-choice questions that call for a single response and a brief text-based explanation to justify that choice. The other questions are open response items. These address a range of comprehension strategies and skills. Students can revisit the passage to find the evidence they need to answer each question. All questions share the goal of ensuring that students engage in close reading of the text, grasp its key ideas, and provide text-based evidence in their answers. In addition, the questions are formatted to reflect the types of questions that will be asked on standardized tests. The questions generally proceed from easier to more complex:

* The **least challenging** questions call for basic understanding and recall of details. They involve referencing the text verbatim or paraphrasing it. This kind of question might also ask students to identify a supporting detail an author did or did not include when making a persuasive argument.

* The **mid-level** questions call upon students to use mental processes beyond basic recall. To answer these questions, students may need to use context clues to unlock the meaning of unfamiliar words and phrases (including figurative language), classify or compare information, make inferences, distinguish facts from opinions, or make predictions. Such a question might also ask students to summarize the main idea(s) of a passage.

* The **deeper** questions focus on understanding that goes beyond the text. Students may need to recognize the author's tone and purpose, make inferences about the entire passage, or use logic to make predictions. This kind of question might even call upon students to determine why an author began or ended the passage as he or she did.

You may find it useful to have students reference line numbers from the passage for efficiency and clarity when they formulate answers. They can also refer to the line numbers during class discussions. Provide additional paper so students have ample space to write complete and thorough answers.

An answer key (pages 76–80) includes sample answers based on textual evidence and specific line numbers from the passage that support the answers. You might want to review answers with the whole class. This approach provides opportunities for discussion, comparison, extension, reinforcement, and correlation to other skills and lessons in your current plans. Your observations can direct the kinds of review and reinforcement you may want to add to subsequent lessons.

About the Teaching Notes

Each passage in this book is supported by a set of teaching notes found on pages 13–25.

In the left column, you will see the following features for each set of teaching notes.

❋ Grouping (**Literature** or **Informational Text**) and the genre or form of the piece.

❋ **Focus** statement describing the essential purpose of the passage, its main features, areas of emphasis, and what students will gain by reading it.

❋ **Teaching Tips** to help you motivate, support, and guide students before, during, and after reading. These easy-to-use suggestions are by no means exhaustive, and you may choose to add or substitute your own ideas or strategies.

- **Before Reading** tips include ways to introduce a passage, explain a genre, present a topic, discuss a format, introduce key vocabulary, or put a theme in context. A tip may suggest how to engage prior knowledge, connect with similar materials in other curriculum areas, or build motivation.

- **During Reading** tips offer possible procedures to help students work through the text, ideas for highlighting key words or concepts, suggestions for graphic organizers, and so on.

- **After Reading** tips provide follow-up questions, discussion topics, extension activities, further readings, or writing assignments linked to the text.

In the right column, are the essential CCSS connections for the passage sorted according to the specific sections of the document: **RL** (Reading Standards for Literature) or **RI** (Reading Standards for Informational Text), **W** (Writing Standards), and **L** (Language Standards). The CCSS chart on page 12 provides the correlations for the entire book at a glance and a URL for the CCSS website where you can find the specific wording of each skill.

Under the essential CCSS connections, you will find a **Complexity Index**, which offers analytical information about the passage based on the three aspects of text complexity, briefly summarized on the next page.

✳ **Quantitative** value, represented by a Lexile score.

✳ **Qualitative** rating, which appears in a matrix that presents four aspects of this measure:

- **Meaning** for literary texts (single level of meaning ↔ multiple levels of meaning) or **Purpose** for informational texts (explicitly stated purpose ↔ implicit purpose)

- **Structure** (simple ↔ complex organization; simple ↔ complex graphics)

- **Language** (literal ↔ figurative; clear ↔ ambiguous; familiar ↔ unusual; conversational ↔ formal)

- **Knowledge** (life experience; content expectations; cultural or literary background needed)

Each of the above aspects are ranked from 1 to 5, briefly summarized, as follows:

1	2	3	4	5
Simple, clear text; accessible language, ideas, and/or structure	Mostly linear with explicit meaning/purpose; clear structure; moderate vocabulary; assumes some knowledge	May have more than one meaning/purpose; some figurative language; more demanding structure, syntax, language, and/or vocabulary; assumes some knowledge	Multiple meanings/purposes possible; more sophisticated syntax, structure, language, and/or vocabulary; assumes much knowledge	May require inference and/or synthesis; complex structure, syntax, language, and/or vocabulary; assumes extensive knowledge

✳ **Reader and Task** considerations comprise two or more bulleted points. Ideas relating to the reader appear first, followed by specific suggestions for a text-based task. Reader and Task considerations also appear embedded within the teaching notes as well as in the guiding question that opens each passage and in the comprehension questions. Keep in mind that Reader and Task considerations are the most variable of the three measures of text complexity. Reader issues relate to such broad concerns as prior knowledge and experience, cognitive abilities, reading skills, motivation by and engagement with the text, and content and/or theme concerns. Tasks are typically questions to answer, ideas to discuss, or activities to help students navigate and analyze the text, understand key ideas, and deepen comprehension. The same task may be stimulating for some students but daunting to others. Because you know your students best, use your judgment to adjust and revise tasks as appropriate.

Teaching Routine to Support Close Reading

Complex texts become more accessible to readers who are able to use various strategies during the reading process. One of the best ways to scaffold students through this process is to model a close-reading routine.

❊ **Preview the text.** Help students learn to identify clues about the meaning, purpose, or goal of the text. They can first read the title and the guiding question that precedes the passage. In literary texts, students can scan for characters' names and clues about setting and time frame. In informational texts, students can use features such as paragraph subheadings and supporting photos, illustrations, or other graphics to get a sense of the organization and purpose.

❊ **Quick-read to get the gist.** Have students do a "run-through" individual reading of the passage to get a sense of it. The quick-read technique can also help students identify areas of confusion or problem vocabulary. You can liken this step to scanning a new store to get a sense of how it is set up, what products it sells, and how you can find what you need.

❊ **Read closely.** Next, have students read the same piece again, this time with an eye to unlocking its deeper meaning or purpose. For most students, this is the time to use sticky notes, highlighter pens, margin notes, or graphic organizers to help them work their way through the important parts of the text. You might provide text-related graphic organizers, such as T-charts, compare/contrast and Venn diagrams, character and concept maps, cause-and-effect charts, or evidence/conclusion tables.

❊ **Respond to the text.** Now it's time for students to pull their ideas together and for you to assess their understanding. This may involve summarizing, reading aloud, holding group discussions, debates, or answering written questions. When you assign the after-reading question pages, suggest that students reread questions as needed before they attempt an answer. Encourage them to return to the text as well. Remind students to provide text-based evidence as part of every answer. Finally, consider with students the big ideas of a piece, its message, lesson, or purpose, and think about how to extend learning.

Above all, use the passages and teaching materials in this book to inspire students to become mindful readers—readers who delve deeply into a text to get the most out of it. Help your students recognize that reading is much more than just decoding all the words. Guide them to dig in, think about ideas, determine meaning, and grasp messages.

   The following page presents three copies of a reproducible, six-step guide to mindful reading. It is intended as a reusable prompt. Students can keep it at hand to help them recall, apply, and internalize close-reading strategies whenever they read.

25 Complex Text Passages To Meet the Common Core: Literature and Informational Texts, Grade 5 © 2014 by Scholastic Teaching Resources

How to Be
A Mindful Reader

Preview the text.
- Set a purpose for reading.

Read carefully.
- Slow down and stay focused.
- Monitor your understanding.

Read again.
- You might notice new information.

Take notes.
- Mark difficult words or phrases.
- Write questions in the margin.
- Make connections between ideas.

Summarize.
- Add headings.
- Jot down the main ideas.
- List the events in sequence.

Think about it.
- Read between the lines. What's the message?
- Do you agree or disagree?
- Has anything been left out?

How to Be
A Mindful Reader

Preview the text.
- Set a purpose for reading.

Read carefully.
- Slow down and stay focused.
- Monitor your understanding.

Read again.
- You might notice new information.

Take notes.
- Mark difficult words or phrases.
- Write questions in the margin.
- Make connections between ideas.

Summarize.
- Add headings.
- Jot down the main ideas.
- List the events in sequence.

Think about it.
- Read between the lines. What's the message?
- Do you agree or disagree?
- Has anything been left out?

How to Be
A Mindful Reader

Preview the text.
- Set a purpose for reading.

Read carefully.
- Slow down and stay focused.
- Monitor your understanding.

Read again.
- You might notice new information.

Take notes.
- Mark difficult words or phrases.
- Write questions in the margin.
- Make connections between ideas.

Summarize.
- Add headings.
- Jot down the main ideas.
- List the events in sequence.

Think about it.
- Read between the lines. What's the message?
- Do you agree or disagree?
- Has anything been left out?

Connections to the Common Core State Standards

As shown in the chart below, the teaching resources in this book will help you meet many of the reading, writing, and language standards for grade 5 outlined in the CCSS. For details on these standards, visit the CCSS website: www.corestandards.org/the-standards/.

Passage	Reading: Literature								Reading: Informational Text									Reading: Foundational Skills		Writing		Language					
	RL.5.1	RL.5.2	RL.5.3	RL.5.4	RL.5.6	RL.5.7	RL.5.9	RL.5.10	RI.5.1	RI.5.2	RI.5.3	RI.5.4	RI.5.5	RI.5.7	RI.5.8	RI.5.9	RI.5.10	RF.5.3	RF.5.4	W.5.9	W.5.10	L.5.1	L.5.2	L.5.3	L.5.4	L.5.5	L.5.6
1	•	•	•	•			•	•										•	•	•	•	•	•	•	•	•	•
2	•	•	•	•		•	•	•										•	•	•	•	•	•	•	•	•	•
3	•	•	•	•	•	•		•										•	•	•	•	•	•	•	•	•	•
4	•	•	•	•		•		•										•	•	•	•	•	•	•	•	•	•
5	•	•	•	•		•	•	•										•	•	•	•	•	•	•	•	•	•
6	•	•	•	•	•		•											•	•	•	•	•	•	•	•	•	•
7	•	•	•	•	•	•	•	•										•	•	•	•	•	•	•	•	•	•
8	•	•	•	•	•	•		•										•	•	•	•	•	•	•	•	•	•
9	•	•	•	•			•	•										•	•	•	•	•	•	•	•	•	•
10									•	•	•	•	•		•		•	•	•	•	•	•	•	•	•	•	•
11									•	•	•	•			•		•	•	•	•	•	•	•	•	•	•	•
12									•	•	•	•	•	•	•	•	•	•	•	•	•	•	•	•	•	•	•
13									•	•	•	•	•		•		•	•	•	•	•	•	•	•	•	•	•
14									•	•	•	•		•	•	•	•	•	•	•	•	•	•	•	•	•	•
15									•	•	•	•	•		•	•	•	•	•	•	•	•	•	•	•	•	•
16									•	•	•	•			•		•	•	•	•	•	•	•	•	•	•	•
17									•	•	•				•		•	•	•	•	•	•	•	•	•	•	•
18									•	•		•			•		•	•	•	•	•	•	•	•	•	•	•
19									•	•	•	•					•	•	•	•	•	•	•	•	•	•	•
20									•	•	•			•	•		•	•	•		•	•	•	•	•	•	•
21									•	•	•			•	•		•	•	•	•	•	•	•	•	•	•	•
22									•	•	•					•	•	•	•	•	•	•	•	•	•	•	•
23									•	•	•			•	•		•	•	•	•	•	•	•	•	•	•	•
24									•	•	•	•		•	•	•	•	•	•	•	•	•	•	•	•	•	•
25									•	•	•			•		•	•	•	•	•	•	•	•	•	•	•	•

Passage 1 — Troubled Times • page 26

Literature: Historical Fiction

▶ **Focus** In this story, students examine elements of plot, setting, and character as they read about a formative period in American history.

▶ **Teaching Tips**

Before Reading

- Provide background about the Revolutionary War. Link with social studies curriculum.

During Reading

- Have students highlight words or phrases the author uses to build tension and suspense.
- Help students identify and distinguish patriots/rebels from loyalists to the British crown.

After Reading

- Ask students to compare and contrast this story with other examples of historical fiction of the American Revolutionary period.

Common Core Connections

RL.5.1, RL.5.2, RL.5.3, RL.5.4, RL.5.9, RL.5.10 • RF.5.3, RF.5.4 • W.5.9, W.5.10 • L.5.1, L.5.2, L.5.3, L.5.4, L.5.5, L.5.6

Complexity Index

Quantitative: Lexile 880

Qualitative	1	2	3	4	5
Meaning		✳			
Structure		✳			
Language		✳			
Knowledge			✳		

Reader & Task

- Students may lack knowledge of the historical context in which this piece is set, and may need guidance to link the characters with their allegiances.
- Have students highlight details in the story that they could later confirm by research.

Passage 2 — Odysseus and Polyphemus • page 28

Literature: Myth

▶ **Focus** By reading the retelling of part of *The Odyssey*, students learn about a clever solution to a seemingly impossible problem, in which brain triumphs over brawn.

▶ **Teaching Tips**

Before Reading

- Tell students that this story comes from an epic Greek work that is over 3,000 years old (Homer's *The Odyssey*). Pronounce the names: Odysseus [oh-DIS-yus], Polyphemus [pol-ə-FEE-mus], Cyclops [SY-klops], Zeus [zus].

During Reading

- Encourage students to form mental images to aid comprehension and assist memory.

After Reading

- Have students summarize and retell this story.
- Extend by helping students learn how Odysseus and his men escaped from the cave.

Common Core Connections

RL.5.1, RL.5.2, RL.5.3, RL.5.4, RL.5.7, RL.5.9, RL.5.10 • RF.5.3, RF.5.4 • W.5.9, W.5.10 • L.5.1, L.5.2, L.5.3, L.5.4, L.5.5, L.5.6

Complexity Index

Quantitative: Lexile 880

Qualitative	1	2	3	4	5
Meaning		✳			
Structure		✳			
Language			✳		
Knowledge			✳		

Reader & Task

- Most students will be motivated to read a heroic tale of men versus a threatening monster.
- Challenge students to read closely to identify the traits that make Odysseus a successful leader.

Literature: Fable

▶ **Focus** This descriptive retelling of an Aesop fable challenges readers to grasp a classic problem and the meaning of the concluding moral.

▶ **Teaching Tips**

Before Reading
- Engage prior knowledge of fables from Aesop and other cultural traditions.
- Review the characteristics of a fable and its concluding lesson or moral.

During Reading
- Encourage students to read the fable quickly to get a sense of it, then reread it more slowly and carefully to absorb the details.

After Reading
- Have students summarize the fable and its moral in their own words. Challenge them to write a modern-day version (no mice and cat) to fit the moral.

Common Core Connections

RL.5.1, RL.5.2, RL.5.3, RL.5.4, RL.5.6, RL.5.7, RL.5.9, RL.5.10 • RF.5.3, RF.4.4 • W.5.9, W.5.10 • L.5.1, L.5.2, L.5.3, L.5.4, L.5.5, L.5.6

Complexity Index

Quantitative:
Lexile 890

Qualitative	1	2	3	4	5
Meaning		✳			
Structure		✳			
Language	✳				
Knowledge	✳				

Reader & Task

- Most students will be familiar with the structure of an Aesop fable.
- Have students compare and contrast the characters of the young mouse and old mouse, and explain the differences.

Literature: Humorous Story

▶ **Focus** This anecdote gives students the opportunity to explore characters' motivations and reactions to the unexpected, and to identify elements of humor and colorful idioms.

▶ **Teaching Tips**

Before Reading
- Preview some challenging vocabulary in this tale, such as *guffawed, collaborators, brimmed, nettled, gaggle, giddy, festooned, garish,* and *bewildered.*

During Reading
- Encourage readers to imagine themselves as guests at Charlie's party.

After Reading
- Discuss the photo. Have students identify the character it represents and explain their reasoning. Have them compare and contrast it with typical birthday party photos.
- Extend by having small groups read the piece aloud in Reader's Theater style.

Common Core Connections

RL.5.1, RL.5.2, RL.5.3, RL.5.4, RL.5.7, RL.5.10 • RF.5.3, RF.4.4 • W.5.9, W.5.10 • L.5.1, L.5.2, L.5.3, L.5.4, L.5.5, L.5.6

Complexity Index

Quantitative:
Lexile 900

Qualitative	1	2	3	4	5
Meaning		✳			
Structure		✳			
Language			✳		
Knowledge		✳			

Reader & Task

- Some students may struggle with the challenging vocabulary, figurative language, and idiomatic expressions.
- Have students make margin notes to identify text, actions, or responses that surprise or puzzle them as the story unfolds.

Literature: Epic Story

▶ **Focus** This retelling of a Hindu epic challenges students to read on two levels: to grasp the literal events of the story and to infer the deeper symbolic meaning it conveys.

▶ **Teaching Tips**

Before Reading
- Clarify for students that an *epic* is a long story-poem, usually written about heroic themes. This passage is a prose retelling of part of a major Hindu epic poem.
- Durga is a key figure in Hindu culture. Have students keep this is mind as they read.

During Reading
- Suggest that students complete a plot diagram to help them track characters, conflicts, events, and outcomes in the story.

After Reading
- Have students compare and contrast Mahisha and Durga. Use a T-chart to which students can contribute traits, descriptions, and values.
- Extend by having students learn about common customs of annual *Durga Puja* festivals.

Common Core Connections

RL.5.1, RL.5.2, RL.5.3, RL.5.4, RL.5.7, RL.5.9, RL.5.10 • RF.5.3, RF.5.4 • W.5.9, W.5.10 • L.5.1, L.5.2, L.5.3, L.5.4, L.5.5, L.5.6

Complexity Index

Quantitative: Lexile 910

Qualitative	1	2	3	4	5
Meaning				✻	
Structure		✻			
Language			✻		
Knowledge			✻		

Reader & Task

- Most students may find the dramatic battle exciting, while some may feel uneasy about the fighting.
- Tell students that this piece is more than a war story. Have groups discuss what some of its deeper meanings may be.

Literature: Folktale

▶ **Focus** This Gullah folktale (from the Georgia Sea Islands) offers students an opportunity to identify foreshadowing to make predictions about what may happen, and to compare and contrast characters by their actions and attitudes.

▶ **Teaching Tips**

Before Reading
- Review the characteristics of folktales.
- Present background on Gullah culture and the unique traits of the Georgia Sea Islands.

During Reading
- Guide readers to highlight words or phrases that foreshadow (hint at) things to come (for example, Mama Snail's warning).

After Reading
- Have students discuss what the ending of the folktale reveals about Snail.

Common Core Connections

RL.5.1, RL.5.2, RL.5.3, RL.5.4, RL.5.6, RL.5.9, RL.5.10 • RF.5.3, RF.5.4 • W.5.9, W.5.10 • L.5.1, L.5.2, L.5.3, L.5.4, L.5.5, L.5.6

Complexity Index

Quantitative: Lexile 930

Qualitative	1	2	3	4	5
Meaning			✻		
Structure		✻			
Language		✻			
Knowledge			✻		

Reader & Task

- Some students may lack the maturity or insight to recognize imbalance in the friendship.
- Have students track evidence to support the differences between Snail and Crab.

Literature: Short Story

▶ **Focus** This story, with many tall-tale elements, requires students to distinguish reality from absurdity to appreciate its surprise ending.

▶ **Teaching Tips**

Before Reading
- Discuss elements of humor used in this tale, such as irony, absurdity, and understatement.

During Reading
- Encourage students to consult a dictionary for challenging words whose meanings they cannot fully discern from context.

After Reading
- Have students create a character sketch of Max, the talking dog.
- Extend by inviting volunteers to read the story aloud with dramatic flair, as a stand-up comedian might.

Common Core Connections

RL.5.1, RL.5.2, RL.5.3, RL.5.4, RL.5.6, RL.5.7, RL.5.9, RL.5.10 • RF.5.3, RF.5.4 • W.5.9, W.5.10 • L.5.1, L.5.2, L.5.3, L.5.4, L.5.5, L.5.6

Complexity Index

Quantitative: Lexile 940

Qualitative	1	2	3	4	5
Meaning			✳		
Structure		✳			
Language				✳	
Knowledge			✳		

Reader & Task

- Some students may lack the necessary questioning skills to grasp the absurdity of this tale. Others may enjoy it and retell it to friends and family members.
- Have students analyze the story to explain its effectiveness.

Literature: Realistic Fiction

▶ **Focus** Readers explore setting, character relationships, types of conflict, and the values of friendship, flexibility, and support.

▶ **Teaching Tips**

Before Reading
- Inform students that child actors must attend school while they are filming a movie or TV show. Clarify that most follow the curriculum used at schools back home and have lessons and do homework between acting requirements.

During Reading
- Provide T-charts for students to compare and contrast regular classrooms with on-set ones, typical students with child-actor students, and regular teachers with on-set teachers.

After Reading
- Divide students into groups of four. Have them assume the roles of the three characters and a narrator, and perform the story in Reader's Theater style.

Common Core Connections

RL.5.1, RL.5.2, RL.5.3, RL.5.4, RL.5.6, RL.5.7, RL.5.10 • RF.5.3, RF.5.4 • W.5.8, W.5.9, W.5.10 • L.5.1, L.5.2, L.5.3, L.5.4, L.5.5, L.5.6

Complexity Index

Quantitative: Lexile 950

Qualitative	1	2	3	4	5
Meaning			✳		
Structure			✳		
Language				✳	
Knowledge				✳	

Reader & Task

- Most students will be unfamiliar with the particular challenges faced by child actors and their on-set teachers.
- Have students describe, compare, and contrast the relationships among the three characters in this story.

Literature: Legend

▶ **Focus** Readers examine the elements of a scary story that characterize it as a legend.

▶ **Teaching Tips**

Before Reading

- Review the characteristics of a legend, such as its links to the past, its unexplained or exaggerated events, its possible connection to actual events, and the likelihood that its telling may have changed over time.
- Point out Cape Cod's location on a map and provide some background on the area.

During Reading

- Encourage readers to highlight sensory details that enhance the tale's macabre nature.

After Reading

- Invite volunteers to act as storytellers and present the tale as if they were telling it around a campfire. Students might add sound effects to enhance the scary details.
- Extend by having students create a note that the young sailor might have left in the shack.

Common Core Connections

RL.5.1, RL.5.2, RL.5.3, RL.5.4, RL.5.9, RL.5.10 • RF.5.3, RF.5.4 • W.5.9, W.5.10 • L.5.1, L.5.2, L.5.3, L.5.4, L.5.5, L.5.6

Complexity Index

Quantitative: Lexile 1010

Qualitative	1	2	3	4	5
Meaning				✳	
Structure			✳		
Language			✳		
Knowledge				✳	

Reader & Task

- Most students will find a scary story engaging and motivating.
- Have students imagine themselves as one of the Grants and attempt to explain what they experienced.

Passage 10 — Two Into One • page 44

Informational Text: Linguistics Article

▶ **Focus** Students integrate information from an assortment of text and graphical features to understand a linguistics concept.

▶ **Teaching Tips**

Before Reading
• Have students first scan the page to notice its many components.

During Reading
• Help students pronounce difficult words.
• Ask students to start a list of portmanteau words they find in the passage. Have them add to it over time.

After Reading
• Read the poem "Jabberwocky" aloud. Ask students to identify its portmanteau words, and then work together to try to determine how each was formed.

Common Core Connections

RI.5.1, RI.5.2, RI.5.3, RI.5.4, RI.5.5, RI.5.8, RI.5.10 • RF.5.3, RF.5.4 • W.5.9, W.5.10 • L.5.1, L.5.2, L.5.3, L.5.4, L.5.5, L.5.6

Complexity Index

Quantitative:
Lexile 880

Qualitative	1	2	3	4	5
Purpose		✳			
Structure				✳	
Language			✳		
Knowledge			✳		

Reader & Task

• ELL students may have difficulty with the concepts in this lesson. Others may be challenged by the visual variety on the page.
• Have students refer to and link the different sources of information in this article to summarize and explain portmanteau words.

Passage 11 — They Fought Like Cornered Buffalo • page 46

Informational Text: History Essay

▶ **Focus** Students gather details, draw conclusions, and determine author's purpose in this essay about a historically unique unit of American soldiers.

▶ **Teaching Tips**

Before Reading
• Preview some challenging terms: *hallowed ground, cavalry, infantry, reconstituted, desolate, stationed, western frontier, unenviable, subduing, poachers,* and *legacy.*

During Reading
• Have students fill in a graphic organizer with answers to the W questions: who, what, where, when, why.

After Reading
• Compile a list of questions students listed in their answers to question 5. Encourage interested students or groups to do further research to answer as many as they can.

Common Core Connections

RI.5.1, RI.5.2, RI.5.3, RI.5.4, RI.5.8, RI.5.10 • RF.5.3, RF.5.4 • W.5.9, W.5.10 • L.5.1, L.5.2, L.5.3, L.5.4, L.5.5, L.5.6

Complexity Index

Quantitative:
Lexile 890

Qualitative	1	2	3	4	5
Purpose			✳		
Structure			✳		
Language				✳	
Knowledge				✳	

Reader & Task

• Students may not only lack familiarity with Buffalo Soldiers, but may lack the maturity or insight to appreciate their historical significance.
• Have students discuss the significance of the Buffalo Soldiers' contributions. Guide them to consider the historical context and prevailing societal views.

"Just Like Her" • page 48

Informational Text: Memoir

▶ **Focus** Students gain insight into a young dancer's character and motivations by reading direct quotations from her personal recollections.

▶ **Teaching Tips**

Before Reading
- Ask students to locate the African nation of Sierra Leone on a world map or globe.
- Clarify that text presented in italics are the subject's own words.

During Reading
- Have students highlight important or influential events, actions, or attitudes that shaped Michaela's life after being orphaned.

After Reading
- Have students list questions they want to research to learn more about Michaela DePrince.
- If possible, show the 2011 documentary film *First Position* to students (or view clips readily available online). Discuss the emotions Michaela conveys as she dances.

Common Core Connections

RI.5.1, RI.5.2, RI.5.3, RI.5.4, RI.5.5, RI.5.7, RI.5.8, RI.5.9, RI.5.10 • RF.5.3, RF.5.4 • W.5.9, W.5.10 • L.5.1, L.5.2, L.5.3, L.5.4, L.5.5, L.5.6

Complexity Index

Quantitative: Lexile 900

Qualitative	1	2	3	4	5
Purpose	❈				
Structure		❈			
Language		❈			
Knowledge			❈		

Reader & Task

- Many students will be inspired by reading this real-life "rags-to-riches" memoir.
- Challenge students to confirm details Michaela describes by doing research online and sharing their findings with classmates.

Savvy Shopper • page 50

Informational Text: Technical Writing/Comparing Data

▶ **Focus** This piece challenges students to read both text and data closely to compare and contrast ingredients and nutrition facts for similar products.

▶ **Teaching Tips**

Before Reading
- Tell students that U.S. health regulations require food products to include information about the ingredients they include and the nutrition they provide. Tell them they will familiarize themselves with the conventions of a nutrition label with this selection.

During Reading
- Suggest that students compare and contrast the nutritional information line by line or item by item as they read to identify differences between the two cereals.

After Reading
- Have students research the three components of foods we eat: carbohydrates, fats, and proteins. Have them list foods that represent each category.

Common Core Connections

RI.5.1, RI.5.2, RI.5.3, RI.5.4, RI.5.5, RI.5.8, RI.5.10 • RF.5.3, RF.5.4 • W.5.9, W.5.10 • L.5.1, L.5.2, L.5.3, L.5.4, L.5.5, L.5.6

Complexity Index

Quantitative: Lexile 910

Qualitative	1	2	3	4	5
Purpose			❈		
Structure				❈	
Language				❈	
Knowledge			❈		

Reader & Task

- Students may be challenged by the format and layout of the data, as well as the number of scientific words included in the nutrition labels.
- Ask students to discuss the advantages and/or disadvantages of having detailed nutrition information on food products.

Informational Text: Word Origin Essay

▶ **Focus** In this essay, students learn about the unexpected historical origins of some common English words and expressions.

▶ **Teaching Tips**

Before Reading
- Ask students what a grease monkey is (mechanic). Tell them that this term once had an entirely different meaning.

During Reading
- Encourage students to reread each paragraph to reinforce comprehension and retention.

After Reading
- Have students use dictionaries and/or online etymology sites to determine the logging-related meaning of the additional lumber lingo examples in the sidebar.

Common Core Connections

RI.5.1, RI.5.2, RI.5.3, RI.5.4, RI.5.7, RI.5.8, RI.5.9, RI.5.10 • RF.5.3, RF.5.4 • W.5.9, W.5.10 • L.5.1, L.5.2, L.5.3, L.5.4, L.5.5, L.5.6

Complexity Index

Quantitative: Lexile 910

Qualitative	1	2	3	4	5
Purpose		✳			
Structure			✳		
Language			✳		
Knowledge			✳		

Reader & Task

- Students may not yet know that language changes all the time, and that words and expressions may once have had different meanings.
- Have students summarize the main theme of this essay, and explain the origins of the logging words and phrases presented.

Informational Text: Literary Fan Letter

▶ **Focus** By reading this response to a novel, students learn about the letter writer as well as the famous author and his classic adventure story.

▶ **Teaching Tips**

Before Reading
- Brainstorm books students have read that touched them deeply. Invite them to explain what the book meant to them.

During Reading
- As students read, have them jot down each paragraph's main idea in the margin.

After Reading
- Discuss the issue Tyler raises about using animals as main characters in a realistic adventure story. Have students share their views on this question.

Common Core Connections

RI.5.1, RI.5.2, RI.5.3, RI.5.4, RI.5.8, RI.5.9, RI.5.10 • RF.5.3, RF.5.4 • W.5.9, W.5.10 • L.5.1, L.5.2, L.5.3, L.5.4, L.5.5, L.5.6

Complexity Index

Quantitative: Lexile 930

Qualitative	1	2	3	4	5
Purpose			✳		
Structure		✳			
Language		✳			
Knowledge			✳		

Reader & Task

- Some students may have little interest in reading a response to a book they haven't read, one that was written so long ago, or one that concerns a topic beyond their experience.
- Have students evaluate the impact upon Tyler of reading *Call of the Wild* and learning about its author.

One-of-a-Kind Museum • page 56

Informational Text: Museum Review

▶ **Focus** Students analyze a reviewer's response to a visit to a unique museum.

▶ **Teaching Tips**

Before Reading
- Draw attention to the title of the review and invite students to predict what they will be reading about.
- Clarify that MoMath is the official nickname for The National Museum of Mathematics.

During Reading
- Encourage students to reread sentences, pause to process new information, make margin notes with questions to discuss, and consult a dictionary as needed.

After Reading
- Revisit the quotation from Glen Whitney in line 3. Help students explain what Whitney meant. Discuss whether MoMath may be able to influence people's attitudes toward math.

Common Core Connections

RI.5.1, RI.5.2, RI.5.3, RI.5.4, RI.5.7, RI.5.8, RI.5.10 • RF.5.3, RF.5.4 • W.5.9, W.5.10 • L.5.1, L.5.2, L.5.3, L.5.4, L.5.5, L.5.6

Complexity Index

Quantitative: Lexile 940

Qualitative	1	2	3	4	5
Purpose			✳		
Structure		✳			
Language				✳	
Knowledge				✳	

Reader & Task

- Some students may not understand the titles or descriptions of some of the museum's activities. However, most will grasp that the writer is enthusiastic about them.
- Have students describe how a museum review can benefit readers, visitors, and the museum itself.

To Buckle Up or Not? • page 58

Informational Text: Persuasive Essay

▶ **Focus** Students must sort fact from opinion as they read and analyze a well-constructed persuasive essay on a controversial topic.

▶ **Teaching Tips**

Before Reading
- Review the features of a well-constructed persuasive essay, such as an engaging opening, point-by-point arguments supported with details, acknowledgement of opposing views, and a strong closing that summarizes the writer's position.

During Reading
- Have students pause after reading each paragraph to identify its main idea and specific purpose in the overall argument presented. Encourage them to jot down key words or questions they have in the margins.

After Reading
- With students, generate a Fact versus Opinion chart, based on the examples they listed to answer question 5. Encourage debate and discussion.

Common Core Connections

RI.5.1, RI.5.2, RI.5.3, RI.5.4, RI.5.8, RI.5.10 • RF.5.3, RF.5.4 • W.5.9, W.5.10 • L.5.1, L.5.2, L.5.3, L.5.4, L.5.5, L.5.6

Complexity Index

Quantitative: Lexile 950

Qualitative	1	2	3	4	5
Purpose			✳		
Structure			✳		
Language			✳		
Knowledge			✳		

Reader & Task

- Students may be aware of this issue, but are unlikely to be familiar with the presentation of a logically organized argument.
- Have students evaluate the logic and effectiveness of the arguments presented, and whether they support the writer's conclusion.

Informational Text: Biographical Sketch

▶ **Focus** Students blend biographical details and direct quotations to understand a renowned woman's character, motivation, and reputation.

▶ **Teaching Tips**

Before Reading

• Preview the title, paragraph subheadings, and photo to motive students to learn about an unusual historical character.

During Reading

• Encourage students to use context clues to determine the meaning of unfamiliar words or phrases. Point out that such clues often appear later in a paragraph.

• As needed, link the antiquated word *ruction* (line 29) with *ruckus* to aid comprehension.

After Reading

• Tell students that there are countless tales about Calamity Jane, but few that can be verified beyond doubt. Challenge interested students to seek out stories of her exploits to share with classmates.

Common Core Connections

RI.5.1, RI.5.2, RI.5.3, RI.4.4, RI.5.8, RI.5.10 • RF.5.3, RF.5.4 • W.5.9, W.5.10 • L.5.1, L.5.2, L.5.3, L.5.4, L.5.5, L.5.6

Complexity Index

Quantitative: Lexile 960

Qualitative	1	2	3	4	5
Purpose				✳	
Structure			✳		
Language				✳	
Knowledge				✳	

Reader & Task

• Some students may lack sufficient background knowledge of 19th-century American pioneer life to appreciate how unique and surprising a woman Calamity Jane was.

• Have students write a brief summary of the significant details of Calamity Jane's life that support her colorful reputation.

Informational Text: Anthropology Essay

▶ **Focus** Students must read carefully and critically to comprehend and draw conclusions about how new anthropological data has affected earlier theories.

▶ **Teaching Tips**

Before Reading

• Brainstorm what students already know or have heard about the earliest people to live in North America.

• Preview the passage by reading its title, subheadings, and opening question. Discuss how some of the subheadings suggest uncertainty.

During Reading

• Have students pause after each paragraph to review its key ideas and important details and jot down questions in the margins.

• As needed, clarify key ideas, such as anthropology, peopling, and first arrivals.

After Reading

• Discuss questions students formulated during reading. Challenge interested students to research how scientists establish reasonable estimates of the age of ancient objects.

Common Core Connections

RI.5.1, RI.5.2, RI.5.3, RI.4.4, RI.5.7, RI.5.8, RI.5.10 • RF.5.3, RF.5.4 • W.5.9, W.5.10 • L.5.1, L.5.2, L.5.3, L.5.4, L.5.5, L.5.6

Complexity Index

Quantitative: Lexile 960

Qualitative	1	2	3	4	5
Purpose					✳
Structure			✳		
Language				✳	
Knowledge				✳	

Reader & Task

• The information in this essay may challenge some students' beliefs or their abilities to rationally reflect on concepts of prehistoric life and migration.

• Have students summarize the key points of this essay by creating an anthropological timeline and annotating it accordingly.

Informational Text: Art History Essay

▶ **Focus** This essay guides students to recognize cause-and-effect relationships between an idealistic but tumultuous historical period and the art that emerged from it.

▶ **Teaching Tips**

Before Reading
- Preview examples of inspirationally beautiful as well as ominous paintings and photos by the artists mentioned in the essay. Invite students' observations.
- As needed, review the historical climate before and during America's Civil War.

During Reading
- Have students read the entire piece quickly to get a general sense of its challenging ideas. Then have them reread it slowly to grasp cause-and-effect relationships.

After Reading
- Revisit the art students viewed before reading. Ask them to reconsider their understanding of the works in light of what they read in the essay.

Common Core Connections

RI.5.1, RI.5.2, RI.5.3, RI.5.4, RI.5.7, RI.5.8, RI.5.10 • RF.5.3, RF.5.4 • W.5.9, W.5.10 • L.5.1, L.5.2, L.5.3, L.5.4, L.5.5, L.5.6

Complexity Index

Quantitative:
Lexile 970

Qualitative	1	2	3	4	5
Purpose					✳
Structure			✳		
Language				✳	
Knowledge					✳

Reader & Task

- The complexity of the topic requires critical and analytical skills that some students may struggle with. Use online art gallery sites to enhance understanding.
- Have students discuss how and why artists might choose to show fear or anxiety in a beautiful work of art.

Informational Text: Technology Article

▶ **Focus** Students explore cause-and-effect and problem-and-solution links to follow an idea from inception to implementation.

▶ **Teaching Tips**

Before Reading
- Brainstorm smartphone apps students know or use. Talk about those that offer assistance regarding health and safety concerns.
- Identify *hackathon* as a portmanteau word (hacker + marathon).

During Reading
- Suggest that as students read, they highlight evidence about problem-solution details in one color and cause-effect links in another color.

After Reading
- Preview the website www.rodedog.com. If appropriate for your students, have them visit it to see an interview with Victoria Walker and to learn more about the current status of the Rode Dog app.

Common Core Connections

RI.5.1, RI.5.2, RI.5.3, RI.5.4, RI.5.7, RI.5.8, RI.5.10 • RF.5.3, RF.5.4 • W.5.9, W.5.10 • L.5.1, L.5.2, L.5.3, L.5.4, L.5.5, L.5.6

Complexity Index

Quantitative:
Lexile 980

Qualitative	1	2	3	4	5
Purpose			✳		
Structure			✳		
Language			✳		
Knowledge			✳		

Reader & Task

- Students are likely to connect with this upbeat real-life story about a young student's clever idea to address a familiar and serious safety issue.
- Have students infer the nature of the relationship between Victoria and her mother, and how it led to Victoria's success.

Informational Text: Procedural/Science Activity

▶ **Focus**   Students read and follow a detailed set of instructions for building a working model of a pinhole camera.

▶ **Teaching Tips**

Before Reading

• Inform students that the human eye is a type of camera; light enters through a small opening in the eyeball and the brain flips and interprets the image to make sense of it.

During Reading

• Encourage students to read the instructions several times. The first reading can be to get a general idea of the project. Subsequent readings should be slow and careful to ensure understanding of each step and the cumulative step-to-step connections.

After Reading

• Have students apply these instructions to build pinhole cameras.
• Discuss the outcome of students' efforts to build pinhole cameras: Which steps were the most challenging? What might have benefitted from more details or visual examples?

Common Core Connections

RI.5.1, RI.5.2, RI.5.3, RI.5.4, RI.5.10 • RF.5.3, RF.5.4 • W.5.9, W.5.10 • L.5.1, L.5.2, L.5.3, L.5.4, L.5.5, L.5.6

Complexity Index

Quantitative:
Lexile 990

Qualitative	1	2	3	4	5
Purpose			✳		
Structure			✳		
Language			✳		
Knowledge					✳

Reader & Task

• Students may have had little experience following detailed instructions to create a working model of something.
• Challenge students to create a timeline of the history of photography.

Informational Text: Newspaper Article

▶ **Focus**   Students grasp the essential meaning of an idiom by understanding how a project that combines compassion, ingenuity, and music can improve people's lives.

▶ **Teaching Tips**

Before Reading

• Present the term *philharmonic* (from the Greek for "loving harmony") orchestra to help students recognize the pun within the subheading Landfill Harmonic.
• Discuss what it means to transform something.

During Reading

• Encourage students to link the photo with the text to better understand the title and the idiom that opens the piece.

After Reading

• If appropriate for your class, together watch trailers for the documentary *Landfill Harmonic*, which can be seen online (for example, at www.landfillharmonicmovie.com).
• Discuss students' thoughts and reactions.

Common Core Connections

RI.5.1, RI.5.2, RI.5.3, RI.5.4, RI.5.7, RI.5.8, RI.5.10 • RF.5.3, RF.5.4 • W.5.9, W.5.10 • L.5.1, L.5.2, L.5.3, L.5.4, L.5.5, L.5.6

Complexity Index

Quantitative:
Lexile 990

Qualitative	1	2	3	4	5
Purpose				✳	
Structure			✳		
Language			✳		
Knowledge				✳	

Reader & Task

• Some students may lack the maturity or compassion to recognize that trash-picking is a sad necessity, not a chosen way of life.
• Help students think deeply about the realities of life in so poor a place as Cateura, and discuss how Favio Chavez's vision can impact the lives of so many there and elsewhere.

Informational Text: Food History/Cultural Essay

▶ **Focus** Students gather information about Spanish tapas through text, a photo, and sidebar features.

▶ **Teaching Tips**

Before Reading
- Have students scan the page to notice the different ways information is presented.

During Reading
- Have students summarize the main idea of each paragraph before going on to the next.
- Ask students to keep in mind the difference between tapas (the food) and sharing tapas (a social experience).

After Reading
- Invite students to describe finger-food snacks typical of their cultures.
- Extend by having students research tapas recipes, or hold a tapas tasting in which they prepare some of the simple recipes they find.

Common Core Connections

RI.5.1, RI.5.2, RI.5.3, RI.5.4, RI.5.7, RI.5.8, RI.5.10 • RF.5.3, RF.5.4 • W.5.9, W.5.10 • L.5.1, L.5.2, L.5.3, L.5.4, L.5.5, L.5.6

Complexity Index

Quantitative:
Lexile 1000

Qualitative	1	2	3	4	5
Purpose			✳		
Structure			✳		
Language			✳		
Knowledge				✳	

Reader & Task

- Even students who have no familiarity with Spain or its culinary traditions are likely to be motivated to read about food.
- Have students analyze how the title fits the essay, focusing on how a basic snack has grown in stature.

Passage **25**   **Seeds for the Future** • page 74

Informational Text: Botany Article

▶ **Focus** In this botany article, students follow a reasoned argument, determine cause-and-effect relationships, and make predictions.

▶ **Teaching Tips**

Before Reading
- Tell students that farmers throughout history have saved seeds for later use.
- Preview challenging science vocabulary: *Millennium, facility, species, climate change, habitat destruction, extinct, regenerate,* and *drought-resistant.*

During Reading
- Have students skim the piece first to get a sense of its organization, structure, and main ideas. Then have them reread more closely to assimilate the information.

After Reading
- Have students write a summary of what the Millennium Seed Bank botanists do and why they do it.

Common Core Connections

RI.5.1, RI.5.2, RI.5.3, RI.5.4, RI.5.8, RI.5.10 • RF.5.3, RF.5.4 • W.5.9, W.5.10 • L.5.1, L.5.2, L.5.3, L.5.4, L.5.5, L.5.6

Complexity Index

Quantitative:
Lexile 1010

Qualitative	1	2	3	4	5
Purpose				✳	
Structure				✳	
Language					✳
Knowledge					✳

Reader & Task

- Some students may lack the maturity and broader world view required to appreciate the importance of the Millennium Seed Bank project.
- Discuss why some scientists focus on the future when we face so many scientific challenges today.

Name _____ Date _____

Troubled Times

How did the rebellion affect the McCrea family?

1 The steady downpour began in the afternoon. But the relentless rain was
2 not the most dismal of the day's news in Rutland, at least not for the McCrea
3 family. For early that morning, after kissing Janey and little Ben, Daniel
4 hugged his worried wife and joined Colonel Seth Warner and his militia
5 men. They were on their way across the river to the fighting.
6   Times were hard on everyone. It was the autumn of 1777, and General
7 Burgoyne and his Indian allies were on the move, marching south from
8 Ticonderoga. All townspeople were scared, and not only of the invading
9 British army. Tense neighbors were at each other's throats; they couldn't
10 trust one another, as some were for the rebellion, like the McCreas, while
11 others were loyal to the crown.
12   After supper that night, the McCreas were huddled by the warmth of their
13 kitchen fire, quietly consumed by their thoughts. The rain had tapered off
14 and it was still outside, when, suddenly, the sound of clopping horse's hooves
15 outside broke the silence and seized their full attention. The sound stopped
16 abruptly but was then followed by the stomping of boot heels on their porch
17 and then a vigorous rapping on their door. It was Will Dunn, from over in
18 Hubbardton, and he was in a frenzy.
19   "Ellie, Ellie, take the children to your cellar! Hurry!" he barked. "There's
20 a raiding party of Redcoats not twenty miles from here and they've got
21 Iroquois for company. Do it now! I must go." With that, Will Dunn tipped
22 his soggy cap, hustled out, and galloped off to his next dire call. The McCrea
23 family hurriedly grabbed blankets, lifted the trap door, and dropped down
24 into the musty darkness.
25   They waited in breathless terror for
26 what seemed like hours when they heard
27 dogs barking and men shouting. Within
28 moments, the clamor of a rumbling
29 stampede had passed. But they soon heard
30 boot steps above, then nothing, and then
31 saw the alarming glow of a lantern shining
32 from the trap door. Mother, daughter,
33 and son were paralyzed with fear when a
34 familiar voice called down to them.
35   "It's me. The bridges are out so we've
36 had to come back," Daniel McCrea calmly
37 said as he leaned his craggy face near to
38 his family. "The British can't cross either.
39 Everyone's safe for now."

25 Complex Text Passages to Meet the Common Core: Literature and Informational Texts, Grade 5 © 2014 by Scholastic Teaching Resources

Name _____ Date _____

Troubled Times

▶ **Answer each question. Give evidence from the historical fiction.**

1 Which word could replace *dire* (line 22) without changing the meaning of the sentence?

  ○ A. local   ○ B. hurried   ○ C. urgent   ○ D. entertaining

How did you determine your response? _____

_____

_____

2 Which best describes who General Burgoyne was?

  ○ A. a rebel leader   ○ C. an Iroquois chief

  ○ B. a British officer   ○ D. a McCrea family friend

What evidence in the text helped you answer? _____

_____

_____

3 Who is Ellie? Explain how you know. _____

_____

_____

_____

4 What could explain why the bridges were out (line 35)? _____

_____

_____

5 How does the author build suspense in this story? _____

_____

_____

_____

_____

Name _____ Date _____

Odysseus and Polyphemus
Greek Myth (From *The Odyssey*)

How does Odysseus use his wits to solve a terrifying problem?

1   On a distant island, Odysseus and his soldiers discovered
2   an enormous cave with lambs, young goats, and great
3   wheels of cheese. The curious travelers ate while awaiting the
4   shepherd. They had skins of wine to exchange for hospitality.
5   Tinkling bells at dusk announced the returning shepherd
6   and his flock. Directing his animals into the cave was a
7   giant—a Cyclops with one monstrous eye in the center of his
8   forehead. Shocked at tiny strangers enjoying his cheese, he
9   roared, "Daring intruders, who are you?"
10   "We are Greeks soldiers returning from war," Odysseus
11 replied. "The laws of Zeus demand you to offer us kindness
12 and generosity."
13   Outraged, the Cyclops rolled a massive boulder to block the cave.
14 "I, Polyphemus, obey NO laws on MY island! You are uninvited pirates,
15 although possibly tasty." With that he snatched two startled men and
16 gobbled them down, slurping in loud satisfaction.
17   The stunned soldiers wailed, "O Zeus, spare us from this cruel destiny!"
18 But Polyphemus just yawned. Odysseus considered killing Polyphemus as he
19 slumbered, but realized that this would leave them entombed in the cave.
20 While the men mourned their lost companions, Odysseus devised a strategy.
21   At dawn, before leading his flock to pasture and obstructing the exit,
22 Polyphemus munched two men for breakfast. Then Odysseus and the
23 soldiers feverishly planned the details of their escape.
24   Polyphemus returned that night to a courteous welcome. "Charming
25 Cyclops, let us no longer be enemies," cooed Odysseus. "I offer you this gift
26 of ambrosial wine, superior to what the gods enjoy on Mount Olympus.
27 Please, drink your fill."
28   Sipping the wine, Polyphemus exclaimed, "Best I've ever had! Tell me your
29 name, little man."
30   "My friends and enemies address me as Nobody," stated Odysseus.
31   "Then Nobody you are and will eternally be after I eat you. But to respect
32 your offering, I'll save you for last," Polyphemus answered. He devoured two
33 more unlucky soldiers, guzzled the wine, and was soon snoring.
34   Quietly, Odysseus clutched a stick from the fire and plunged its red-hot
35 end into the monster's eye. The brute's agonized shrieks brought his Cyclops
36 neighbors at once. "What's wrong?" they yelled.
37   "Nobody has invaded my cave and Nobody has blinded me!" screamed
38 Polyphemus. Assuming that their friend was having a nightmare, the
39 Cyclops neighbors shrugged and left. …

Name _____ Date _____

Odysseus and Polyphemus

▶ **Answer each question. Give evidence from the myth.**

1 How did Odysseus and his soldiers learn that the shepherd was returning?

○ A. They smelled the animals.   ○ C. They felt the earth tremble.

○ B. They heard him whistling.   ○ D. They heard the sound of bells.

How did you determine your response? _____

_____

_____

2 Which best describes what the soldiers believed would be their *destiny* (line 17)?

○ A. They would be eaten alive.   ○ C. They would outsmart the Cyclops.

○ B. They would enjoy a lavish feast.   ○ D. Most of them would escape unharmed.

What evidence in the text helped you answer? _____

_____

_____

3 Describe a Cyclops. _____

_____

_____

4 Why did Odysseus act so welcoming of Polyphemus on the second night? Explain. _____

_____

_____

_____

5 What was so clever about the name Odysseus chose to tell Polyphemus? _____

_____

_____

Name _____ Date _____

Belling the Cat

Fable by Aesop

What makes it so difficult for the mice to solve their problem?

1 Mice and cats have been the bitterest of enemies for as long as anyone
2 can recall. So how is it that the swift and clever mice never found a way
3 to control their opponent? This age-old tale may guide you to understand
4 the depth of the problem.

5 Long ago, a cat in one town was especially successful at attacking the
6 local mice. Fearing for their future, the anxious mice decided to gather
7 for a crucial meeting. Their goal was to devise a strategy to outsmart their
8 feline enemy. Every mouse willingly attended, and hopes were high.

9 Many mice addressed the crowd, each with a different idea for their
10 protection and safety. But no idea seemed to satisfy the group. At last a
11 young mouse arose to speak to the crowd. "My friends, I wish to offer a
12 new proposal. As I see it, our biggest problem is the sly manner in which
13 the cat advances toward us. If we could receive a signal of its sneaky
14 approach, we would likely escape. So I recommend that we obtain a
15 small bell that makes a clear ring. We simply hang the bell from a strong
16 cord and then tie that cord around the cat's neck. From that moment
17 onward, any movement the cat makes will cause the bell to ring. Thanks
18 to our good ears, the bell will warn us when our enemy nears. It should
19 provide ample warning to keep us safe and out of sight."

20 This new idea drew loud cheers until an elderly gray mouse slowly
21 stood up. "We must commend our young friend for a highly original
22 idea. But before we charge ahead, I must pose one simple question. Who
23 among us volunteers to be the one to bell the cat?"

24 The mice looked embarrassed and uneasy. Complete silence overtook
25 the group.

26 **MORAL:** *It is one thing to say that something should be done,*
27 *but quite a different matter to do it.*

Name _____ Date _____

Belling the Cat

▶ **Answer each question. Give evidence from the fable.**

1 Which of the following animals is a *feline* (line 8)?

○ A. rat   ○ B. hawk   ○ C. leopard   ○ D. old mouse

How did you determine your response? _____

_____

_____

2 Which is another way to state the lesson that this fable teaches?

○ A. Trouble comes from the direction we least expect it.   ○ C. Necessity is the mother of invention.

○ B. It is easy to suggest impossible remedies.   ○ D. Slow and steady wins the race.

What evidence in the text helped you answer? _____

_____

_____

_____

3 According to the young mouse, what characteristic behavior of the mouse-eating cat makes it so especially dangerous?

_____

_____

4 Explain in your own words the problem with the young mouse's idea. _____

_____

_____

_____

5 Why did "complete silence" overtake the group after the old mouse's question (line 24)?

_____

_____

_____

Name _____ Date _____

Charlie's Party

What might explain the prank Jumani played?

1   When Jumani hatched his idea, Luther guffawed and heartily approved.
2   The collaborators planned it for Friday after school. All middle-school
3   teachers, except Charlie, got secret invitations.
4   At Berenice's Bakery, Jumani selected a festive cake. At Party Planners, he
5   chose its tackiest party favors. He brimmed with mischievous anticipation.
6   At 3:15, Luther located Charlie busy at work in the library, whispered
7   to him that the principal had announced a last-minute faculty meeting,
8   and that his attendance was required. Nettled, Charlie closed his laptop
9   and reluctantly accompanied Luther to where the meeting was to be held.
10   When they arrived, Charlie's annoyance turned to puzzlement.
11   "Surprise!" yelled a gaggle of beaming, party-hat-wearing colleagues.
12   The giddy group was clustered around a meeting table festooned with a
13   garish orange birthday cake, hastily wrapped packages, and ridiculous
14   party decorations. "Happy Birthday, Charlie!" Jumani yawped.
15   "But it isn't my birthday," Charlie objected, flashing a crooked,
16   bewildered smile.
17   Luther had anticipated denial, and was on it like frosting on a cupcake.
18   "Come on, Charlie, lose the modesty."
19   "Feliz cumpleaños, Carlos!" chirped Marisol.
20   Others followed suit, and Charlie
21   succumbed, reluctantly taking a seat.
22   Gag gifting, cake eating, and story-telling
23   followed, all in good humor. Then Jumani,
24   wearing an impish expression, told everyone
25   that he had concocted the celebration merely
26   for fun, that it was not really Charlie's
27   birthday. Luther sheepishly confessed his part,
28   too. Some nervous laughter followed, and
29   after a long pause…"I rescheduled a doctor
30   appointment for this, you jerk!" howled Eva.
31   "You knuckleheads! I paid my sitter extra
32   so I could attend this farce!" added Lydia.
33   "This is the last time I listen to you two
34   morons!" Omar barked. He had postponed a
35   key meeting.
36   Ears and cheeks aflame, Jumani vowed
37   never again to mess with someone's birthday.
38   But anniversaries, he thought, might be a
39   horse of another color.

Name _____ Date _____

Charlie's Party

▶ **Answer each question. Give evidence from the story.**

1 Why was Charlie bewildered when he arrived at the meeting place?

○ A. Not all teachers were there.　　　○ C. He didn't understand Spanish.

○ B. It wasn't really his birthday.　　　○ D. He was a shy and modest person.

What evidence in the text helped you answer? _____

_____

_____

2 How did Charlie react when he was summoned to a last-minute meeting?

○ A. annoyed　　　○ B. excited　　　○ C. impish　　　○ D. resigned

How did you determine your response? _____

_____

_____

3 When and where did the party take place? _____

_____

4 List three clues that suggest Jumani is planning a prank. _____

_____

_____

_____

_____

5 How did Jumani respond to the negative reactions from Eva, Lydia, and Omar? _____

_____

_____

_____

_____

Name _____ Date _____

Triumphant Goddess
Hindu Epic Story

What lessons does this epic battle teach?

1 Mahisha, the ferocious buffalo
2 demon, believed he could never be
3 defeated or killed. Feeling invincible,
4 Mahisha commanded his demon army
5 into battle to conquer the entire world
6 and defeat all the gods. Some of the
7 threatened alerted their greatest leaders
8 and beseeched them for help. They
9 responded by creating the stunningly
10 beautiful 8-armed goddess Durga. All
11 the gods gave Durga their weapons,
12 and the mountain god gave her a lion
13 to provide her transportation.
14 Durga became more powerful than all the gods put together. Still, the
15 gods knew that it was decreed that no male could ever defeat the terrible
16 Mahisha. So they hoped that the red-robed goddess would do battle with the
17 buffalo demon herself. Durga agreed to the deed, and the gods blessed her
18 with courage and success.
19 Mahisha heard the great clamor and went to investigate. He came
20 upon the magnificent Durga astride a golden lion. Enticed by her majesty,
21 Mahisha instantly asked Durga to marry him. But instead of accepting his
22 proposal, Durga roared her fierce challenge—a battle to the death.
23 Durga's insulting and daring refusal enraged Mahisha to conquer the
24 willful goddess. Thus began the terrible combat between the archrivals.
25 Mahisha first lunged to kill Durga's lion. Furious, Durga threw a noose
26 over Mahisha, but he had the ability to change his shape at will. He became
27 a lion himself, so Durga lopped his head off. He then became a sword-
28 wielding giant, but Durga pierced him with arrows. Mahisha changed into
29 an elephant and yanked Durga's lion with his trunk, but she sliced off the
30 trunk. The demon hurled mountains at the goddess, who dodged every one.
31 Crazy with power and fury, Mahisha retook his buffalo form.
32 Inspired by the frenzy of battle, Durga stomped on Mahisha's neck and
33 punctured it with her trident. The wily demon began to emerge from his
34 own mouth. Durga immediately sliced off his head, finally destroying
35 Mahisha forever.
36 All the gods rejoiced when the buffalo demon finally fell. They praised
37 Durga, who promised to protect them for all eternity. Thus did good triumph
38 over evil.

Name _____ Date _____

Triumphant Goddess

▶ **Answer each question. Give evidence from the epic story.**

1 Feeling *invincible* (line 3), Mahisha believed that he _____.

    ◯ A. could never be convinced of anything   ◯ C. could never be overpowered

    ◯ B. would one day be conquered   ◯ D. should rule the world

How did you determine your response? _____

_____

_____

2 Each year, Hindus around the world celebrate a major festival known as *Durga Puja* to honor the goddess. Which best explains the meaning of this festival?

    ◯ A. It celebrates the victory of good over evil.   ◯ C. It respects the value of teamwork.

    ◯ B. It honors women who solve problems.   ◯ D. It is a tribute to skill in battle.

What evidence in the text helped you answer? _____

_____

_____

3 Describe the plan the gods devised to defend themselves and the world against Mahisha. Include details designed to make the plan a success.

_____

_____

_____

4 Durga used a trident to battle with Mahisha. Use word-study skills to determine what a *trident* might look like. Explain your thinking and make a simple sketch.

_____

_____

5 What was insulting and daring in Durga's response to Mahisha's marriage proposal? _____

_____

_____

Name _____ Date _____

Mismatched Friends
Gullah Folktale (From the Georgia Sea Islands)

In what ways are the two friends mismatched?

1   Crab and Snail were unlikely friends on account of Snail always being
2   so slow and lagging behind. Snail offered, "You lead the way whilst I watch
3   your back and warn you of danger, like friends do." Crab rolled his bulging
4   eyes to accept this arrangement.

5   One day Crab invited Snail to explore a nearby sandy beach. Snail
6   recalled how sternly his mama always warned him with the mournful tale of
7   Papa Snail getting plucked off the beach by a hungry seagull, nevermore to
8   return. So Snail wisely refused Crab's offer.

9   Crab mocked his friend as a big baby. "Aren't you brave enough to take
10 some chances? How 'bout you walk in front for a change, and I'll watch
11 *your* back and alert *you* to danger." Trusting Crab's friendship, Snail finally
12 agreed and the two ventured off.

13 The beach was glorious to Snail, but his worry made him move more
14 slowly than ever. Crab nudged Snail to enjoy himself. Once Snail relaxed, he
15 began exploring the newfound sights. In his excitement, he never realized
16 that he was walking the beach alone. Near some artful driftwood, Snail
17 turned to thank Crab for this memorable adventure—just as he spotted a
18 seagull diving toward him at great speed. Snail froze, too terrified even to
19 squeeze into his hard shell. His mama's warning echoed in his mind, but it
20 was too late! The bird scooped him up and flew off.

21 Meanwhile, Crab was hiding in a shallow hole he'd quickly dug upon
22 spotting the gull. He'd never warned Snail; Crab simply saved his own
23 crusty self.

24 After dark, Crab dashed from the hole into the sea to break the awful
25 news to Snail's mama. At Snail's hole, Crab clacked his claws wildly. When
26 Snail himself appeared, Crab fainted! He awoke to find Snail and Mama
27 Snail beside him. "I thought you were
28 lost, my friend. It's fantastic to see you,
29 but how did you escape?"

30 Snail replied coolly, "When the
31 kindly She-Gull snatched me, she asked,
32 'Didn't your mama ever tell you to
33 avoid danger?' Ashamed, I admitted
34 that my mama had warned me often,
35 but that I disobeyed."

36 "That's it?" asked Crab.

37 "And She-Gull strongly urged me to
38 find better friends."

25 Complex Text Passages to Meet the Common Core: Literature and Informational Texts, Grade 5 © 2014 by Scholastic Teaching Resources

Name _____ Date _____

Mismatched Friends

▶ **Answer each question. Give evidence from the folktale.**

1 Why does Mama Snail always tell the story of Papa Snail?

⃝ A. She wants Snail to notice when seagulls look hungry.

⃝ B. She hopes Snail will learn about dangers on the beach.

⃝ C. Snail loves when his mother tells him scary stories.

⃝ D. That one is her favorite story.

How did you determine your response? _____

_____

_____

2 Which of the following words could replace *crusty* in line 23 without changing the meaning of the sentence?

⃝ A. sharp   ⃝ B. generous   ⃝ C. experienced   ⃝ D. ill-tempered

What evidence in the text helped you answer? _____

_____

_____

3 Why was Snail reluctant to explore the beach at first? _____

_____

_____

4 Contrast the characters of Crab and She-Gull. _____

_____

_____

5 Reread the opening paragraph. What view of friendship does each character reveal? _____

_____

_____

Name _____ Date _____

The Talking Dog

What is funny about the dog owner's explanation?

1   Kerry was driving through a rural part of Montana when she came upon
2   an undistinguished diner in a small town that the Interstate bypassed. A sign
3   out front announcing "Talking Dog for Sale" caught her eye. She parked in
4   the lot, entered the woebegone eatery, and took a seat at the empty counter.
5   "I see that you have a talking dog for sale," she said to the man who
6   approached her from behind the counter.
7   "I do indeed," he replied and then whistled in the direction of some booths
8   hugging a far wall. "Over here, Max!" he called. A medium-sized hound
9   immediately lifted its head up from one of them, jumped down, scampered
10 over to where Kerry was sitting, and perched himself on an adjacent stool.
11   "You can talk?" she asked.
12   "Can I ever!" Max answered. "I speak so well that I've made quite a
13 handsome living from it. Why, I've worked the world over—Europe, Asia,
14 Africa, mountains, deserts, under water—you name it. In fact, I'm so
15 extraordinarily verbal that I've been in the employ of the FBI and the CIA in
16 a number of critical covert operations."
17   "The FBI? The CIA? Really?"
18   "You'd better believe it, sister. I can proudly assert that I've infiltrated a
19 host of hostile groups, listened quietly and intently to their conversations
20 while reclining under tables or curled up in corners pretending to be
21 snoozing. *Psst; they all thought I was some dumb dog.* When I was back at
22 the office, I communicated precisely what I'd learned to generals and State
23 Department higher-ups." With that, Max took a long slurp from a bowl of
24 water his owner had placed before him, jumped down from his stool, and
25 trotted back to the comfort of his booth.
26   "Wow!" Kerry exclaimed. She stared,
27 completely taken aback, at the man
28 behind the counter. "Max is amazing!
29 How much do you want for him?"
30   "Ten dollars," came the casual reply.
31   "Ten dollars? Why so cheap?"
32 inquired a puzzled Kerry.
33   "Why? Because he's one darned liar,
34 that's why," the man answered. "He's
35 never been anywhere, ever. Spends all
36 his time sprawled out in the yard or
37 snoring in one of my booths!"

Name _____ Date _____

The Talking Dog

▶ **Answer each question. Give evidence from the story.**

1 Which is mostly likely to be *adjacent* (line 10) to a couch?

○ A. a laundry basket   ○ B. a bed   ○ C. a carpet   ○ D. an end table

How did you determine your response? _____

_____

_____

2 A *woebegone* (line 4) dog house would probably benefit most from a _____.

○ A. paint job   ○ B. bigger dog   ○ C. welcome mat   ○ D. shady location

What evidence in the text helped you answer? _____

_____

_____

3 Why did Kerry stop at the diner? _____

_____

_____

_____

4 Describe elements of this story that are like elements of a tall tale. _____

_____

_____

_____

_____

5 What makes the last paragraph of the story so funny? Explain. _____

_____

_____

_____

Name _____ Date _____

School on the Set

What about a classroom like this one would be unusual and challenging?

1   "Must we begin science right now?" Luke ignored Jed's routine question,
2 rolling his eyes unconvincingly. He'd heard it all before—for each subject,
3 every day, at all times. Luke recognized that Jed was far more invested in
4 his number of close-ups than in his education. "Gotta memorize my lines,
5 all million of them," Jed added, wagging his script dramatically in the air.
6   Luke squeezed out a practiced smile and delivered his standard speech.
7 "Jed, this trailer is school, just like the institutions your friends attend
8 back home. School is in session now, exactly as it must be three hours per
9 day, five days per week. Your movie shoot is history for the moment, and
10 you're currently off-set. So yes, we're commencing a stimulating physics
11 lesson today, and I expect you to focus as attentively as you would if the
12 clapper sounded and the director yelled 'Action!' Let's wait for Abigail to
13 arrive, though."
14   "Sir! Yessir!" snapped Jed, in character as the son of a Marine colonel
15 from his previous film. He stood stiffly at attention while he and Luke
16 laughed and saluted like goofy comedians. Abigail, still wearing thick
17 make-up and in costume, lumbered into the trailer, interrupting the little
18 comedy. Making no eye contact, she slumped onto a couch, staring down
19 in heavy silence.
20   "What's up, Abigail?" asked Jed with knowing concern.
21   "Nothing."
22   "Nothing, my foot, Abby," Jed snapped, flopping down beside her.
23 "I may not know physics, but I read body language like the professional
24 I am. You're way upset, girl, so tell Dr. Jed everything that went down."
25   Abigail reluctantly raised her head, inhaling deeply and theatrically.
26 "I've just wrapped my most emotional scene so far. Really heavy stuff, like
27 a woolen cloak burying my head." With that, Abby's eyes shut and tears
28 dripped onto her clenched fists.
29   "I hear you, milady," Jed acknowledged.
30 "Cinema isn't the real thing, but it's still a
31 mighty challenge to change gears on a dime.
32 Even our finest divas couldn't do better."
33   Luke sighed, checked his watch, and
34 gently offered, "Suppose we shelve the
35 physics lesson for now to give Abby time
36 to debrief."
37   "Grand idea, simply awesome," Jed added,
38 "but what's the lesson topic, anyway?"
39   Saying nothing, Luke gestured to his
40 recent posting on the white board.

inertia

1. [Newton's First Law of Motion] objects in motion tend to stay in motion, and objects at rest tend to stay at rest until or unless acted upon by a force;

2. tendency for a person to remain inert or inactive

25 Complex Text Passages to Meet the Common Core: Literature and Informational Texts, Grade 5 © 2014 by Scholastic Teaching Resources

Name _____ Date _____

School on the Set

▶ **Answer each question. Give evidence from the story.**

1 Who is Luke?

○ A. a teacher   ○ B. a script writer   ○ C. an acting coach   ○ D. the owner of a trailer

What evidence in the text helped you answer? _____

_____

_____

2 In line 6, Luke gave a *practiced* smile because he _____.

○ A. wants his students to like him   ○ C. has put great effort into smiling brightly

○ B. has an easy-going sense of humor   ○ D. has responded to Jed this way many times before

How did you determine your response? _____

_____

_____

3 Explain what you learn about Jed by reading that he was "far more invested in his number of close-ups than in his education" (lines 3 and 4).

_____

_____

_____

4 What does the writer imply by calling Abigail's quiet a "heavy silence" (line 19)? _____

_____

_____

5 What is the relationship between the lesson Luke had planned and the situation in the trailer that day?

_____

_____

_____

Name _____ Date _____

Dark and Stormy Night
Cape Cod Legend

What details of this story develop its mystery and scary atmosphere?

1   Mr. and Mrs. Grant were driving past the dunes late one turbulent night
2   in 1923, trying to make it home safely through a raging storm. When their
3   car suddenly broke down, they found themselves stranded near a rickety
4   shack. They wrapped their coats tightly around themselves, hurried to
5   the shack, banged on its door, but got no answer. They peeked through a
6   cracked window whose broken shutters clattered in the gusty wind. Straining
7   their eyes, all they could see was one shabby room with three lopsided chairs
8   and a sagging bed. Everything lay covered under a thick blanket of dust.
9   Realizing the dangers of struggling by foot through the fierce winds and
10 rain, the couple decided to take shelter for the night in that sorry shack.
11 They figured they would deal with the car the next day. Carrying in blankets
12 from the car, they left footprints in the dust as they settled in. Soon they were
13 fast asleep.
14   At midnight, the Grants both sat bolt upright in bed. A thin young sailor,
15 dripping wet, stood by the stone-cold fireplace as if drying himself. His skin
16 had a green glow in the darkness. Mrs. Grant nervously called, "Who's
17 there?" The sailor coughed and vanished.
18   Thinking they were dreaming, the Grants went back to sleep. Next
19 morning, they found a salty puddle near the fireplace. Yet they saw no other
20 footprints in the dust but their own.
21   The weather was calm, so they
22 walked to the nearest town for help.
23 A mechanic towed their car to his
24 shop and set to work on it while the
25 Grants waited in the local diner. They
26 struck up conversation with Mrs.
27 Whaley, the owner who had lived in
28 the area her whole life. Upon asking
29 after the shack, the Grants learned
30 that it had been empty for almost
31 40 years. Mrs. Whaley recalled that,
32 after losing their only son at sea, the
33 heartbroken owners moved to Iowa,
34 never to return.

25 Complex Text Passages to Meet the Common Core: Literature and Informational Texts, Grade 5 © 2014 by Scholastic Teaching Resources

Name _____ Date _____

Dark and Stormy Night

▶ **Answer each question. Give evidence from the legend.**

1 Which of the following words is an *antonym* for the word *turbulent* (line 1)?

　○ A. agitated 　　○ B. parched 　　○ C. serene 　　○ D. somber

How did you determine your response? _____

_____

_____

2 Why did Mr. and Mrs. Grant spend the night in the old shack?

　○ A. They were on vacation. 　　　○ C. They planned to meet their son there.

　○ B. They needed shelter in the bad storm. 　○ D. They parked their car in its driveway.

What evidence in the text helped you answer? _____

_____

_____

3 What clue do the Grants' footprints in the dust reveal about the shack? _____

_____

_____

4 Why did the author include the character of Mrs. Whaley? _____

_____

_____

_____

5 What elements of this story help you know that it is a legend? _____

_____

_____

_____

_____

Name _____ Date _____

Two Into One

How do different text features work together to explain an idea?

1 Portmanteau (port-MAN-toe) is a French word for an old type of suitcase
2 with two distinct parts, used to keep items organized and separate. It opened
3 like a book, and some portmanteaus could stand up.
4 Linguists* apply the term portmanteau to any word
5 formed by blending parts of two separate words into one.
6 A portmanteau word folds together the meanings of both
7 words. Consider the word smog. Linguists trace it back to a
8 combination of <u>sm</u>oke and f<u>og</u>. Motel came from the words
9 <u>mot</u>or and h<u>otel</u>.
10 The best portmanteau words eventually
11 make their way into spoken and written
12 language. So how do you recognize this
13 type of word and grasp its meaning?
14 A writer who added many of them to
15 English and a nursery rhyme character
16 can assist you!
17 Best known for his classic Alice's
18 Adventures in Wonderland (1865),
19 author Lewis Carroll enjoyed word
20 play. His sequel to Alice, called Through
21 the Looking-Glass (1871), includes the
22 famous poem "Jabberwocky." After
23 reading it, Alice describes it as "very
24 pretty" but "rather hard to understand."
25 Part of the challenge of understanding
26 this nonsense poem is that Carroll
27 made up many portmanteau words,
28 such as slithy (SLY-thee). Humpty
29 Dumpty explains its meaning to
30 Alice like this:

31 " Well, slithy means 'lithe' and
32 'slimy.' 'Lithe' is the same as
33 'active.' You see it's like a
34 portmanteau—there are two
35 meanings packed up into
36 one word. "

> *** linguist**
> a person who
> studies the history,
> structures, and
> meanings of
> language

37 **Familiar Portmanteau Words**

38	alphabet	=	<u>alpha</u> + <u>beta</u>
39	blog	=	we<u>b</u> + <u>log</u>
40	brunch	=	<u>br</u>eakfast + <u>lunch</u>
41	caplet	=	<u>cap</u>sule + tab<u>let</u>
42	emoticon	=	???? + ????
43	Internet	=	<u>interc</u>onnected + <u>network</u>
44	Muppet	=	<u>m</u>arionette + <u>puppet</u>

Name _____ Date _____

Two Into One

▶ **Answer each question. Give evidence from the article.**

1 A *sequel* (line 20) is a book that _____ another book about the same characters.

○ A. copies   ○ B. reviews   ○ C. comes after   ○ D. comes before

What evidence in the text helped you answer? _____

_____

_____

2 *Linguistics* is the study of _____.

○ A. language   ○ B. lines and angles   ○ C. luggage   ○ D. punctuation

What evidence in the text helped you answer? _____

_____

_____

3 Why is *portmanteau* a logical name for a word formed by parts of two other words?
Use the photograph and text to help you construct your answer.

_____

_____

4 Many people use *emoticons* when they write emails and text messages. Examples include ;-) for a winking smile and :-D for a huge grin. Explain how you think this portmanteau word came about.

_____

_____

5 *Chortle* is another portmanteau word Lewis Carroll created. It is a gleeful way to laugh. Carroll combined part of the word *snort* with part of another word. What do you think that other word was? Explain. You may want to consult a thesaurus to help you.

_____

_____

_____

_____

_____

Name _____ Date _____

They Fought Like Cornered Buffalo

Who were the Buffalo Soldiers and what is their legacy?

1   On September 6, 2005, Mark Matthews was buried in hallowed ground
2 in Arlington National Cemetery. Matthews was 111 when he died. He had
3 been the oldest living Buffalo Soldier.

4 **Began** In 1866, Congress established six new army
5 units—two cavalry* and four infantry** regiments. Soon
6 thereafter, the four infantry units were reconstituted as
7 two. Together with the cavalry units, they were assigned to
8 duty in harsh and desolate posts in the Great Plains and
9 the Southwest. Some of the men were Civil War veterans.
10 Some were former slaves. All were African Americans.
11 They were the first all-black professional soldiers in a peacetime army.
12 Five thousand in number, they constituted about 10 percent of the Federal
13 troops stationed on the western frontier.

> * **cavalry**
> soldiers who fight on horseback
>
> ** **infantry**
> foot soldiers

14 **Nicknamed** The Cheyenne admired their fierceness. They called them
15 *Buffalo Soldiers*, a term of respect. They claimed that the troops fought
16 like those animals when wounded and cornered. They said, too, that the
17 soldiers' hair reminded them of the curly cushion between a buffalo's
18 horns. The name stuck.

19 **Posted** Much of what the Buffalo Soldiers faced was unenviable.
20 Their job included catching outlaws and rustlers, chasing Mexican
21 revolutionaries, escorting mail deliveries, and
22 subduing hostile Native American groups.
23 Furthermore, they were assigned the challenging
24 tasks of mapping unknown lands, establishing
25 outposts for future towns, and constructing roads.
26   The Buffalo Soldiers went on to fight in the
27 Spanish-American War, in Cuba. After the turn
28 of the century, some served as park rangers in
29 California's Yosemite and Sequoia National
30 Parks. There, they evicted poachers and timber
31 thieves. But their main enemy was forest fires.

32 **Honored** Wherever the Buffalo Soldiers served,
33 they served with distinction. Houston's Buffalo
34 Soldier National Museum, founded in 2000, is
35 dedicated to preserving the honor and legacy of
36 these African American heroes.

Name _____ Date _____

They Fought Like Cornered Buffalo

▶ **Answer each question. Give evidence from the essay.**

1 Which of these jobs was *not* assigned to Buffalo Soldiers in the West?

○ A. building roads   ○ B. catching outlaws   ○ C. creating maps   ○ D. hunting buffalo

What evidence in the text helped you answer? _____

_____

_____

2 Cemeteries are not the only examples of *hallowed ground* (line 1). Which of the following locations would most likely be considered hallowed ground?

○ A. an old public library   ○ C. the site of a notable battle

○ B. a large shopping mall   ○ D. a famous baseball stadium

What evidence in the text helped you answer? _____

_____

_____

3 What made the Cheyenne nickname of Buffalo Soldiers a term of respect? _____

_____

_____

4 The Buffalo Soldiers emblem included the words "We can, we will" and "Ready and forward." How does the information given in this essay support these slogans?

_____

_____

_____

5 Now that you have read a brief essay about Buffalo Soldiers, what else would you like to know about them? Draft three questions you might ask.

_____

_____

_____

Name _____   Date _____

"Just Like Her"

What do the dancer's memories reveal about her character?

1 Michaela DePrince (b. 1995) is
2 a professional performer with The
3 Dance Theatre of Harlem. She
4 began life as Mabinty Bangura
5 in the war-torn West African
6 nation of Sierra Leone. Orphaned
7 by age three, she lived for some
8 months in a harsh orphanage.
9 Fortunately, at the age of four,
10 she was unexpectedly adopted by
11 an American family. From that
12 day forward, her life improved
13 dramatically.
14 Michaela shares some
15 recollections about experiences
16 that shaped her.

17 **Earliest Memories** *I don't*
18 *remember much, but it was just*
19 *terrible. I do remember that I lost*
20 *a lot of people that I cared about.*
21 *In the orphanage, I got the least*
22 *amount of food, the worst clothes,*
23 *and the last choice of toys. I had really bad malnutrition, and I was really sick all*
24 *the time—I would've probably died if my parents didn't adopt me.*

25 **Drawn to Dance** *I found a magazine by the orphanage gate. In it I noticed*
26 *a picture of a ballerina wearing a tutu and pointe shoes. She just looked so happy*
27 *and I was in such a terrible place that I thought, if I ever get adopted, maybe I*
28 *could be just like her.*
29 *I'd never seen anything like that before, so I took the cover off and put it in my*
30 *underwear because I had nowhere else to put it. I kept the picture with me every*
31 *day until I got adopted. It kept me believing and looking forward to something.*

32 **Challenges** *I've had my bad patches where I wanted to quit ballet, but I would*
33 *say to myself, this is what I've been dreaming of for so long, I really need to keep*
34 *trying. Nothing else has ever made me feel like that. Dance is a part of who I am,*
35 *and I can't see myself doing anything else.*

Name _____ Date _____

"Just Like Her"

▶ **Answer each question. Give evidence from the memoir.**

1 Who was Mabinty Bangura (line 4)?

⃝ A. She was the person who adopted Michaela.

⃝ B. She was the name Michaela was given at birth.

⃝ C. She was the director of the orphanage in Sierra Leone.

⃝ D. She was the dancer pictured in the magazine Michaela found.

What evidence in the text helped you answer? _____

_____

_____

2 Someone who suffers from *malnutrition* (line 23) _____.

⃝ A. has no parents   ⃝ C. will never be able to succeed in life

⃝ B. was born in another country   ⃝ D. has not been getting enough healthy food

What evidence in the text helped you answer? _____

_____

_____

3 What beliefs helped Michaela overcome challenges as a dancer? _____

_____

_____

4 Michaela recalls being in "such a terrible place" (line 27). How can this comment have two meanings?

_____

_____

5 What can you infer from this piece about the impact the DePrinces had on Michaela's life? Explain.

_____

_____

Name _____ Date _____

Savvy Shopper

How can the way data is presented help or confuse decision-making?

1 There are dozens and dozens of breakfast cereals that line supermarket
2 shelves all around the country. So, how do savvy shoppers pick one that
3 is not only healthy and tasty but also fits the family budget? One way
4 shoppers can begin is to compare nutritional information.
5 Below is some information from the side panels found on most boxes
6 of cereal. There are important details to examine both in the ingredients
7 list and in the nutritional analysis. In this example, both wheat-based
8 products are quite similar: Wheat-Shreds Sweet-n-Frostie Bites appears on
9 the left, and Wheat-Shreds Original Spoonfuls appears on the right. Both
10 cereals are small "pillows" made of woven strands of whole wheat. What
11 distinguishes one cereal from the other? How can shoppers choose?

Carbohydrates

Food

Protein   Fats

Foods have
1, 2, or 3 parts.

Wheat-Shreds Sweet-n-Frostie Bites

NUTRITION FACTS
Serving Size: 21 Biscuits (54g)

Amount Per Serving	Cereal	with 1/2 cup skim milk
Calories	190	230
Calories from Fat	10	10
	% Daily Value	
Total Fat 1g	2%	2%
Saturated Fat 0g	0%	0%
Trans Fat 0g		
Polyunsaturated Fat 0.5g		
Monosaturated Fat 0g		
Cholesterol 0mg	0%	0%
Sodium 0mg	0%	3%
Potassium 200mg	6%	11%
Total Carbohydrate 46g	15%	17%
Dietary Fiber 6g	23%	23%
Soluble Fiber less than 1g		
Insoluble Fiber 5g		
Sugars 1g		
Protein 5g		

INGREDIENTS:
Whole grain wheat, sugar. Contains 2% or less of brown rice syrup, gelatin, BHT for freshness.

Wheat-Shreds Original Spoonfuls

NUTRITION FACTS
Serving Size: 1 cup (49g)

Amount Per Serving	
Calories 170 Calories from Fat 10	
	% Daily Value
Total Fat 1g	2%
Saturated Fat 0g	0%
Trans Fat 0g	
Cholesterol 0mg	0%
Sodium 0 mg	0%
Potassium 170 mg	5%
Total Carbohydrate 40g	13%
Dietary Fiber 6g	24%
Sugars 0g	
Protein 6g	

INGREDIENTS:
Whole grain wheat. To preserve the natural wheat flavor, BHT is added to the packaging material.

25 Complex Text Passages to Meet the Common Core:
Literature and Informational Texts, Grade 5
© 2014 by Scholastic Teaching Resources

Name _____ Date _____

Savvy Shopper

▶ **Answer each question. Give evidence from the data.**

1 How many grams of carbohydrates are in one serving of the Original Spoonfuls cereal?

○ A. 13　　　○ B. 40　　　○ C. 46　　　○ D. 49

What evidence in the text helped you answer? _____

_____

_____

2 It takes a *savvy* shopper to spot differences among products. Which word best describes the decisions savvy shoppers usually make?

○ A. disinterested　　　○ B. foolish　　　○ C. hasty　　　○ D. informed

What evidence in the text helped you answer? _____

_____

_____

3 Compare the ingredients lists of both products. Summarize the differences. _____

_____

_____

_____

4 Suppose someone must follow a low-sugar diet. Which of these cereals would be the better choice? Explain.

_____

_____

5 What is potentially misleading or confusing about comparing the nutritional information presented for these two products?

_____

_____

_____

Name _____ Date _____

Lumber Lingo

How do new words and phrases enter into our language?

1   In the 1850s, settlers poured into Seattle, Washington.
2   Commerce began to boom. The region's rich forests provided
3   lumber for building ships, homes, railroads, and bridges.
4   Lumber was used to build almost anything growing towns
5   needed. Plentiful lumber meant jobs.
6   But making trees into lumber was risky work. It attracted
7   rugged men with steely nerves, great strength, and quick wits.
8   Their work gave rise to colorful terms still used today. It also
9   inspired tales about Paul Bunyan and other folk heroes.
10   *Lumberjacks* (and rare *lumberjills*) did whatever it took to get
11 trees to the mills to be cut. After the jacks felled trees, *buckers*
12 cut them into same-sized logs. Teams of horses, mules, or oxen
13 hauled the logs to town to be processed.
14   Builders in town used some of the logs to make
15 bumpy passageways called *corduroy roads*. Agile
16 *grease monkeys* leapt from log to log, smearing
17 grease on those logs to make them slippery. The
18 corduroy roads acted as crude conveyor belts down
19 which logs rolled easily to the water. From there,
20 they were floated to the mills. Roads used this way
21 were called *skidways*, or *skid roads*.
22   In 1853, Henry Yesler built Seattle's first steam-
23 powered sawmill. This sawmill was able to process
24 more lumber than ever, keeping lumberjacks busier
25 than ever. Mill Road—Yesler's skidway—became
26 known as Skid Row.
27   But in time, new machines and improvements
28 in transportation changed the lumber business.
29 Obsolete skidways were left to rot. Nowadays, the
30 term *skid row* has a different meaning. It describes
31 any rundown or abandoned neighborhood where
32 people down on their luck congregate.

A 19th-century corduroy road

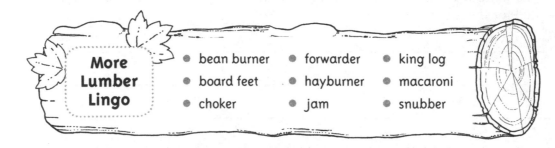

More Lumber Lingo

- bean burner
- board feet
- choker
- forwarder
- hayburner
- jam
- king log
- macaroni
- snubber

Name _____ Date _____

Lumber Lingo

▶ **Answer each question. Give evidence from the essay.**

1 Which industry drew settlers to the Seattle area in the 1850s?

○ A. mining   ○ B. logging   ○ C. shipping   ○ D. road building

What evidence in the text helped you answer? _____

_____

_____

2 Something that has become *obsolete* (line 29) will most likely be _____.

○ A. abandoned   ○ B. preserved   ○ C. repainted   ○ D. up-to-date

What evidence in the text helped you answer? _____

_____

_____

3 How did the work of lumberjacks differ from the work of buckers? _____

_____

_____

4 Think about the theme of this essay. How can it help you understand the meaning of the term *lingo* in the title?

_____

_____

_____

5 Explain why the old-fashioned ways of logging gave rise to folk heroes like Paul Bunyan.

_____

_____

_____

_____

Name _____ Date _____

Thank an Author

What features of the author's work does the writer most appreciate?

1   Dear Jack London,

2   I know that you're not alive to read this letter,
3 and that your most famous books were written
4 a century or so ago. But you are one of my
5 new favorite authors. Most of my friends enjoy
6 reading fantasy and science fiction, maybe some
7 sports stories or a biography now and then.
8 But I like books that tell realistic stories with
9 challenging and unexpected turns. This may
10 seem strange since I've never been anywhere
11 dangerous, and most things in my life are pretty
12 safe and routine.

13   Maybe that's just it. I read *Call of the Wild*
14 while I was recovering from a broken arm. I
15 didn't do anything wild or heroic to break my
16 arm; I just slipped down the stairs and landed
17 badly. But reading your book took me to a
18 distant place, and I couldn't put the book down.

19   The story of Buck's wilderness life was shocking, sad, thrilling, and
20 inspiring at the same time. You made me feel sorry for him, root for him,
21 even dislike him at times. But Buck always felt so real to me, struggling
22 with obstacles in his life. It made my broken arm seem so minor—and that
23 felt good!

24   I read that you never finished high school and traveled around the United
25 States trying to figure out what you wanted to do. You went to Alaska during
26 the great Klondike Gold Rush and experienced hard times there yourself.
27 Maybe that's why Buck comes across as so realistic.

28   Some people argue that an animal has no business being the hero of a
29 realistic story, but I disagree. We don't know for sure what animals think—
30 if they even do. But to me it's a great idea to use an animal to introduce
31 curious readers to bigger ideas, such as loyalty or survival, and using instinct
32 and overcoming hardships.

33   Thank you, Jack London, for a great read. I plan to read *White Fang* next.
34 My mom promises to read me one of your famous short stories, called "To
35 Build a Fire," which is also set in the far north and has a dog in it.

36   Your 21st-century fan,
37 Tyler Hicks

Name _____ Date _____

Thank an Author

▶ **Answer each question. Give evidence from the letter.**

1 Which word is most nearly *opposite* of the word *routine* (line 12)?

○ A. normal   ○ B. expected   ○ C. unscheduled   ○ D. challenging

How did you determine your response? _____

_____

_____

2 Which best explains Jack London's skill and success at writing adventure stories?

○ A. He had little schooling.   ○ C. He lived over a hundred years ago.

○ B. He was no stranger to hard times.   ○ D. He experienced adventures of his own.

What evidence in the text helped you answer? _____

_____

_____

3 What draws Tyler Hicks to Jack London's work? _____

_____

_____

_____

4 What could Tyler mean by saying that reading about Buck "made my broken arm seem so minor" (line 22)?

_____

_____

_____

5 Explain why Tyler might write a fan letter to someone who will never be able to read it.

_____

_____

_____

Name _____ Date _____

One-of-a-Kind Museum

What is unique about MoMath?

1 Glen Whitney believes that studying math is no different than learning
2 how to drive. Anyone can do it! But his concern is that math is too often
3 portrayed as "this forbidden territory, where only initiates can go." So
4 he raised awareness, interest, and money to open The National Museum
5 of Mathematics in New York City. It's the only museum of its kind in the
6 country, and it's mainly for kids. My own three pestered me to check it out.
7 So I made a brief visit to see what the excitement was all about.
8 The stated goal of MoMath is "to stimulate inquiry, spark curiosity, and
9 reveal the wonders of mathematics." It has two floors filled with at least 30
10 unconventional hands-on math activities. When I visited, groups of giddy
11 kids were thoroughly immersed in "Coaster Rollers" and the "Enigma Café."
12 At the "Structure Studio," a gaggle of giggling 6-year-olds were eagerly
13 puttering with architectural toys. And at the "Harmony of Spheres," a trio
14 of girls energetically tapped on colorful, glowing balls. Each ball played a
15 different musical triad. Their spirited "concert" didn't sound particularly
16 melodious to me, but they were clearly having a glorious time.
17 Such lively scenes would delight Glen Whitney. He says that if visitors
18 leave the museum thinking that it was
19 really cool, it would not be the end of
20 his mission, but only the beginning.
21 My visit was only a beginning for
22 me, too. I was so impressed that I
23 plan to take my family there in July
24 for an origami workshop. We'll be
25 folding paper to explore geometric
26 relationships. In the process, we'll
27 create an assortment of beautiful
28 shapes. And in August, we'll attend
29 "Math Encounter: The Cosmic
30 Distance Ladder." It will be a 3-hour
31 investigation of how to use distances
32 we know along with high school math
33 to indirectly measure vast distances
34 between planets, stars, and galaxies.
35 I can't wait!

Origami star

Name _____ Date _____

One-of-a-Kind Museum

▶ **Answer each question. Give evidence from the review.**

1 In what way is MoMath different from all other American museums?

　○ A. It offers workshops.　　　○ C. It focuses only on math.

　○ B. It welcomes children.　　　○ D. It has hands-on activities.

What evidence in the text helped you answer? _____

_____

_____

2 Which word could you substitute for *unconventional* (line 10) without changing the meaning of its sentence?

　○ A. odd　　　○ B. original　　　○ C. irregular　　　○ D. standard ·

What evidence in the text helped you answer? _____

_____

_____

3 What prompted the writer to visit MoMath in the first place? _____

_____

_____

4 How would you describe the writer's reaction to his visit to MoMath? _____

_____

_____

5 Glen Whitney feels that "if visitors leave the museum thinking that it was really cool, it would not be the end of his mission, but only the beginning" (lines 17–20). Explain what he means by this.

_____

_____

_____

_____

Name _____ Date _____

To Buckle Up or Not?

Why are school buses not required to install seat belts for children?

1 **The Issue** In America, all car passengers must wear seat belts, and all
2 cars come with them installed. Yet, although 23 million children ride
3 school buses every weekday, the great majority of the buses transporting
4 them do not have seat belts. They aren't legally required to. Indeed,
5 those in favor of changing the law to make seat belts compulsory face a
6 tough sell. Why is this so?
7   It's not just because kids squirm too much and wouldn't use them
8 correctly. It comes down to two things: design and cost.

9 **Design** Our nation's large, yellow school buses have been designed to
10 be remarkably safe, the safest form of ground transportation we have.
11 For one thing, they are really heavy. In addition, the kids sit high
12 up, above where most collisions take place. Furthermore, all bus
13 seats have high, heavily cushioned backs. Their four inches of
14 thick foam padding absorb impact; they act like air bags. So, in
15 their tightly packed seats, kids are, in effect, sitting in protective
16 bubbles. It should surprise no one that according to statistics
17 compiled by the National Highway Traffic Safety Administration,
18 riding on a large school bus is 40 times safer than riding in a car.

Forty
times
safer!

19 **Cost** Design issues aside, cost issues must be
20 considered, as well. Installing seat belts is very
21 expensive. Doing so would add thousands to the
22 cost of producing each bus, *with minimal, if any,*
23 *impact on safety*. Plus, putting in seat belts would
24 take up space and cause manufacturers to take
25 out seats. With fewer seats in a bus, more buses
26 would be needed.

More
buses =
more
money!

27 **Conclusion** Frankly, although the bus driver should (and does)
28 use one, kids riding a school bus have no need for seat belts. The risk
29 they take in riding them is nowhere near the risk they take each time
30 they approach or leave one. So I agree with what many organizations
31 dedicated to school transportation safety say. I oppose making it
32 mandatory that all school buses be equipped with seat belts.

Name _____ Date _____

To Buckle Up or Not?

▶ **Answer each question. Give evidence from the essay.**

1 Which is *not* a reason the writer gives for why school buses are so safe?

    ◯ A. The buses weigh a great deal.   ◯ C. The seat backs are heavily padded.

    ◯ B. The seats are high above the road.   ◯ D. The buses move slowly and stop often.

What evidence in the text helped you answer? _____

_____

_____

2 Which other word in this essay is a synonym for *mandatory* (line 32)?

    ◯ A. compulsory   ◯ B. expensive   ◯ C. majority   ◯ D. protective

What evidence in the text helped you answer? _____

_____

_____

3 According to the writer, how does the safety of riding in a school bus compare with the safety of riding in a car?

_____

_____

4 What techniques does the writer use to emphasize key points? _____

_____

_____

_____

5 List three examples of facts and three examples of opinions in this essay. _____

_____

_____

_____

_____

Name _____ Date _____

Calamity Jane

How does the author build a case for this celebrated character's nickname?

1   When scout Martha Jane heard the shots, she wheeled
2 her horse around and galloped to the rescue. She caught
3 the wounded soldier just before he fell, hauled him onto
4 her saddle, and rode to safety. Or so she wrote in her
5 autobiography.

Calamity Jane, around 1885

6 **Martha Jane Cannary** Frontier life in America was
7 marked by *calamities*: disasters, disappointments, misfortune,
8 and ruin. Martha Jane Cannary was born in Missouri in
9 1852. During her life, she earned a memorable nickname.
10 Over the years, historians have been able to agree on few
11 verifiable facts about her. Much of what is known may have
12 been exaggerated by writers or embellished by storytellers
13 around campfires. But if even a tenth of her exploits were
14 true, Calamity Jane was a rare individual!

15 **Coming of Age** In 1865, the Cannary family headed west.
16 On their punishing five-month journey, young Martha said
17 she spent most of her time "hunting along with the men and
18 hunters of the parts. I was considered a remarkable good shot
19 and a fearless rider for a girl of my age." By the time she was 15, both her
20 parents had died. Martha raised her two younger brothers and three sisters—
21 clothing, feeding, teaching, and protecting them.
22   To do this, Martha worked as a cook, a nurse, a miner, and an ox-team
23 driver. She recalled, "I was, at all times, with the men when there was
24 excitement and adventures to be had." She swapped her dresses for sturdy
25 frontier buckskin and furs. This hard-living, hard-working woman became a
26 legendary sharpshooter and grouch.

27 **Reputation** Martha's trouble-making reputation was widely known. One
28 old-timer wrote, "[Calamity Jane] got her name from a faculty she has
29 had of producing a ruction at any time and place and on short notice." Or
30 maybe Calamity was just a mocking mispronunciation of her last name.
31 Whichever is true, a common warning at the time was for people to step
32 lightly around her, lest they find themselves "courting calamity." The
33 colorful nickname stuck—and spread.

34 **Rest in Peace** In her 1896 autobiography, Calamity Jane wrote: "As a
35 child I always had a fondness for adventure, outdoor exercise, and especial
36 fondness for horses, which I began to ride at an early age." Calamity Jane
37 died in 1903. Although her life was short in years, it was long in colorful
38 experiences and hair-raising adventures. She is buried in Deadwood, South
39 Dakota, beside her friend, the also-legendary Wild Bill Hickok.

25 Complex Text Passages to Meet the Common Core: Literature and Informational Texts, Grade 5 © 2014 by Scholastic Teaching Resources

Name _____ Date _____

Calamity Jane

▶ **Answer each question. Give evidence from the biographical sketch.**

1 Which of the following words below could you substitute for *faculty* (line 28) without changing the meaning of the sentence?

◯ A. ability ◯ B. failure ◯ C. knack ◯ D. teacher

What evidence in the text helped you answer? _____

_____

_____

2 Why might the "few *verifiable* facts" (lines 10 and 11) about Calamity Jane present a problem for biographers?

◯ A. Calamity Jane had a vivid imagination.

◯ B. Calamity Jane may have been a made-up character.

◯ C. It is difficult to prove some of the claims about her.

◯ D. There are too many facts to decide which ones to use.

What evidence in the text helped you answer? _____

_____

_____

3 What facts of her life forced Martha Jane Cannary to grow up quickly? _____

_____

_____

4 What is the writer's purpose in the opening paragraph of this piece? _____

_____

_____

5 Explain how Martha Jane's life made her such a "rare individual" (line 14). _____

_____

_____

_____

Name _____ Date _____

The Earliest Americans

What factors explain the uncertainty about how and when humans arrived in America?

1 **Out of Africa**   Approximately 100,000 years ago, humans
2 began to spread out from their original homeland in Africa. They
3 started to settle in parts of Asia and Europe. Some even made
4 their way by boat to Australia.
5   If you saw any of them dressed not in animal skins, but
6 in jeans and a T-shirt, they would probably look like your
7 neighbors. But when did these modern humans come here to
8 America? In other words, when was America first peopled?

9 **Peopling America**   *Anthropology* is the study of human beings.
10 Anthropologists believe that humans arrived here sometime
11 within the past 25,000 years. But the researchers haven't been
12 able to agree on precisely when that was. For many years, the
13 accepted view of events was that hunters crossed the Bering Strait
14 from Asia some time during the end of the last ice age, when
15 lowered sea levels had created a land bridge. Those early humans
16 simply walked across. The discovery of points, from spears or
17 arrows, in Clovis, New Mexico, supported this theory. These
18 tools are about 13,500 years old. So that, most anthropologists
19 believed, was about when the first arrivals came to this continent.

Clovis projectile point

20 **Questions Emerge**   However, artifacts subsequently found
21 at other sites across the country appear to be older than the
22 Clovis points. These findings have made some anthropologists skeptical
23 about when the first arrivals actually did get here. Using advanced dating
24 techniques, they have identified artifacts 15,000 and perhaps even 20,000
25 years old. In fact, some researchers have concluded that the first arrivals in
26 America may have come by a different route altogether.

27 **New Theory**   One theory is that they came from Europe. This hypothesis
28 is based on the similarities between artifacts found in states along the east
29 coast and those discovered in southern France and northern Spain between
30 17,000 and 24,000 years ago. Did the first-arriving humans cross the ocean
31 from Europe?

32 **Stay Tuned. . .**   Many anthropologists question the European migration
33 view. In fact, some are unconvinced of the validity of any of the dates of the
34 pre-Clovis discoveries. But it is safe to say that learning more about the first
35 Americans deserves and will get further investigation.

Name _____ Date _____

The Earliest Americans

▶ **Answer each question. Give evidence from the essay.**

1 The major work of anthropologists is to study _____.

○ A. early methods of travel   ○ C. ancient tools and weapons

○ B. the peopling of America   ○ D. the origins and cultures of humankind

What evidence in the text helped you answer? _____

_____

_____

2 An event that happens *subsequently* (line 20) takes place _____.

○ A. at the same time   ○ B. more slowly   ○ C. beforehand   ○ D. afterward

What evidence in the text helped you answer? _____

_____

_____

3 Explain what a *hypothesis* (line 27) is. _____

_____

_____

_____

4 What evidence in the piece supports the idea that travel by boat to America was possible as far back as 25,000 years ago?

_____

_____

_____

5 Explain why some anthropologists question the theory that Clovis points prove that the first arrivals crossed into America by land over the Bering Strait.

_____

_____

_____

Name _____ Date _____

Art of Its Time

In what ways did the Civil War period affect art in America?

1 **Inspiration**   In the mid-19th century, many Americans found the spiritual
2 qualities of the wilderness intriguing. Landscape painting ruled the day.
3 Gifted artists like Frederic Church, Sanford Gifford, George Bingham, and
4 Albert Bierstadt painted nature in all its awesome, pristine beauty. Their
5 canvases celebrated the nation's magnificent mountains and forests. They
6 honored its verdant valleys and unspoiled lakes, from the Catskills in the
7 East to the Sierras in the West. These inspirational paintings represented
8 the boundless opportunities of America. They were hopeful. And they drew
9 thousands westward to experience nature's glory.

10 **Confrontation**   But in 1861, America went to war with itself. The Civil
11 War (1861–1865) was a great catastrophe of the time, and it changed
12 America forever. Magazine illustrators like Winslow Homer and Alfred
13 Waud, and pioneering photographers like Mathew Brady and Alexander
14 Gardner, covered the battles. Their drawings, prints, paintings, and
15 photographs graphically captured the horrors of battle. They brought home
16 the grim reality of war to millions of shocked Americans.

17 **Reflection**   Artists couldn't help being affected by the uneasy, anxious
18 times in which they lived. The turbulence of the nation was represented
19 by Church's stormy, iceberg-strewn waters and violent churning seas.
20 Uncertainty and fear inhabited Gifford's ominous skies, and shadowed
21 Bierstadt's brooding valleys. Moods of mournfulness or alarm made their
22 way onto one canvas
23 after another. The war
24 was never far from
25 artists' thoughts. Art in
26 America reflected the
27 troubled times.

Frederic Edwin Church, *Twilight in the Wilderness*

Name _____ Date _____

Art of Its Time

▶ **Answer each question. Give evidence from the essay.**

1 What did Alfred Waud and Alexander Gardner have in common?

○ A. Both were illustrators.   ○ C. Both covered the Civil War.

○ B. Both were photographers.   ○ D. Both lived in the wilderness.

What evidence in the text helped you answer? _____

_____

2 In the mid-19th century, *pristine* (line 4) land still covered much of America. Which word gives the most accurate description of that kind of landscape?

○ A. unspoiled   ○ B. silent   ○ C. ruined   ○ D. distant

What evidence in the text helped you answer? _____

_____

_____

3 How did Civil War photos and drawings affect Americans? _____

_____

_____

4 The writer describes skies in Gifford's painting as *ominous* (line 20). What do you think Gifford hoped to convey in that scene?

_____

_____

_____

5 Many landscape artists of mid-19th-century America made paintings that were both magnificent and mournful. Explain why this was so.

_____

_____

_____

_____

Name _____ Date _____

Unlikely Hackathon Champ

How can a contest encourage teamwork, innovation, and achievement?

1 When her barking dogs distracted her from a project, Victoria Walker
2 learned an important lesson: sound can be an effective deterrent. The
3 repeated barking prevented the 11-year-old from focusing on her work.
4 Later, when Victoria saw her mom texting while driving, the sixth grader
5 hatched a novel idea.
6 Victoria shared her notion with her mother, a
7 software* designer. Mrs. Walker took Victoria to a
8 technology event where people brainstorm ideas
9 for new software. There, Victoria met David Grau,
10 whose job is to help turn ideas into actual products or
11 services. Victoria had her own idea for a smartphone
12 app. She hoped it could protect her parents who drive
13 and text. Her pitch was simple: "What it does is keep
14 barking at you or making annoying sounds until you
15 turn off your cellphone." Victoria and David teamed
16 up to create that app**.
17 By chance, a major cellphone provider was hosting
18 a two-day contest for software designers to compete
19 to develop new smartphone apps to solve a very real
20 problem. The "It Can Wait" Hackathon offered $20,000 to the innovative
21 team that came up with the best app to discourage people from texting
22 while driving.
23 Victoria's concept and Grau's design became Rode Dog, which won
24 their little team a trip to the finals. Five teams were given ten more days
25 to improve their apps and present them to a panel of judges. In the end,
26 the Rode Dog team won the grand prize. The judges praised Rode Dog,
27 noting that sending barks could be fun. But they valued more Victoria's
28 greater goal: to protect drivers from risky behavior.
29 Since that victory in September of
30 2012, the Rode Dog team has been
31 working to keep improving their
32 app. They now offer other irritating
33 sounds, such as a clucking chicken
34 and a roaring lion. Once they have
35 worked out all the kinks, they will
36 make the app available to users.
37 Victoria tells kids who hope to get
38 involved in technology, "Try your
39 hardest and never give up."

> * **software**
> the set of detailed
> and organized
> steps that make
> a computer
> perform tasks
>
> ** **app**
> (short for application)
> a specialized program
> created to run on
> smartphones.

NO TEXTING
WHILE
DRIVING
ORDINANCE

Name _____ Date _____

Unlikely Hackathon Champ

▶ **Answer each question. Give evidence from the article.**

1 The purpose of any *deterrent* (line 2) is to get people to _____.

○ A. drive more carefully   ○ C. never give up on their dreams

○ B. stop doing something   ○ D. take better care of themselves

What evidence in the text helped you answer? _____

_____

_____

2 What lucky break helped Victoria's idea for an app become real?

○ A. There was a contest for new apps to stop texting while driving.

○ B. Her mother and father texted while they drove.

○ C. David Grau designed irritating noises.

○ D. Her dog had a loud and annoying bark.

What evidence in the text helped you answer? _____

_____

_____

3 What two events did Victoria link that led to her big idea? _____

_____

_____

4 Based on this article, describe what a hackathon is and explain why Victoria became such an unlikely champ.

_____

_____

_____

5 What role did teamwork play in getting Rode Dog from a simple idea to a smartphone app? Explain.

_____

_____

Name _____ Date _____

Making a *Camera Obscura*

How does a pinhole camera work?

1   A *camera obscura* (Latin for "dark room")
2 is the forerunner of the camera and of
3 photography itself. It is a device that
4 projects an image onto a screen without
5 film or power of any kind. You might know
6 this invention as a *pinhole camera*. Here is
7 how to make a simple one:

8   **You will need:**

9   • 2 toilet paper or paper towel tubes   12   • wax paper and black paper
10   • pair of scissors   13   • 1 pin
11   • tape   14   • light source

15   **Steps**

16   **1.** Cut one of the tubes lengthwise so that it unrolls into a rectangle.

17   **2.** Re-roll it, but overlap the ends to form a slightly smaller cylinder, and
18   then tape the ends together. Call this tube #1.

19   **3.** Cut a square of wax paper with sides greater than the diameter of tube
20   #1. Cover one end of the tube entirely with it.

21   **4.** Press the excess wax paper against the outside of the tube. Secure it all
22   the way around with tape. This tube should fit snuggly into the larger
23   tube, called tube #2.

24   **5.** Cut a square of black paper with sides greater than the diameter of
25   tube #2. Cover one end of the tube entirely with it. Press the excess
26   paper against the outside of the tube. Secure it all the way around
27   with tape.

28   **6.** Make one small hole with a pin in the center of the black paper.

29   **7.** Insert tube #1, wax-paper end first, part-way into tube #2.

30   You now have a pinhole camera, a *camera obscura* that you can
31 use! Aim the pinhole end at an object that is well lit by a light bulb or
32 daylight. Look through the open end of tube #1 at the wax paper. Move
33 that tube in and out to focus the image you will see.

Name _____ Date _____

Making a *Camera Obscura*

▶ **Answer each question. Give evidence from the passage.**

1 Which definition of *project* fits its meaning as it is used in line 2?

   ◯ A. stick out   ◯ C. throw a likeness onto

   ◯ B. forecast or predict   ◯ D. plan, proposal, or assignment

What evidence in the text helped you answer? _____

_____

_____

2 What geometric shape is formed by cutting a cylinder lengthwise and unrolling it?

   ◯ A. circle   ◯ B. square   ◯ C. cylinder   ◯ D. rectangle

What evidence in the text helped you answer? _____

_____

_____

3 Why do you think a *camera obscura* is also known as a *pinhole camera*? _____

_____

_____

4 What words would best describe how the image in the *camera obscura* compares with the actual object it is aimed it at?

_____

_____

5 Evaluate this how-to piece for clarity, organization, and effectiveness. What, if anything, might you add, take out, or do differently?

_____

_____

_____

_____

_____

Name _____ Date _____

Transforming Trash

In what ways does the writer explain the idiom about trash and treasure?

1 **Los Reciclados** *One person's trash is another person's treasure.* So says an
2 old idiom. A project that started in a desperately poor slum in Cateura,
3 Paraguay, proves the truth of these words. The musicians of the Paraguay
4 Youth Orchestra have gained hope for the future through the power and
5 joy of making music together. But something rare distinguishes them
6 from other ensembles. All their instruments began as garbage found in
7 the local landfill. This explains their nickname, "The Recycled Orchestra"
8 (*Los Reciclados*).

9 **Favio Chavez** Music teacher and environmentalist Favio Chavez
10 learned to play clarinet and guitar as a child. He was working at a small
11 music school in Paraguay when he got a new job to teach the trash-
12 pickers of Cateura to protect themselves from injury and disease.

13 **Clever Cola** When Chavez observed the terrible
14 living conditions of the local families, he knew he had
15 to help them. So he opened a music school. He had no
16 money, just five old instruments to share among the
17 eager students, and little idea where it all might lead.
18 He soon asked one of the trash-pickers, Cola, to make
19 instruments from found objects. Cola first repaired a
20 broken drum. Then he built a guitar from spare pieces
21 of wood and a flute from tin cans.
22   Favio Chavez always says, "The world sends us
23 garbage. We send back music." The musicians display
24 their instruments with honest pride: a guitar fashioned
25 from two large cans, drums with skins made from old
26 x-rays, a violin whose body was a dented metal bowl.

27 **Landfill Harmonic** As of this writing, Los
28 Reciclados has played in Brazil, Panama, Colombia,
29 and hopes to visit the United States to perform at
30 the Musical Instrument Museum in Arizona. The
31 curator of that museum marvels at "the ingenuity of
32 humans around the world using what they have at
33 their disposal to create music." The documentary film
34 *Landfill Harmonic*, scheduled to open in 2014, will bring
35 this remarkable story to audiences all over the world.

Noelia Rios, 12, tuning her guitar
made of recycled materials

Name _____ Date _____

Transforming Trash

▶ **Answer each question. Give evidence from the article.**

1 Which of the following statements is the most unique fact about *Los Reciclados*?

  ○ A. They plan to visit the United States one day.   ○ C. They are poor children.

  ○ B. Their instruments are made from trash.   ○ D. They live in Paraguay.

What evidence in the text helped you answer? _____

_____

_____

2 Which of the following is an example of *ingenuity* (line 31)?

  ○ A. living in Cateura, Paraguay   ○ C. creating a flute from tin cans

  ○ B. learning to play the clarinet   ○ D. conducting a youth orchestra

What evidence in the text helped you answer? _____

_____

_____

3 What made Favio and Cola such a successful team? _____

_____

_____

4 How does the idiom that begins the article apply to the story of the Paraguay Youth Orchestra? Refer to the title, photo, and text.

_____

_____

_____

5 Write a brief character sketch of Favio Chavez. Use details from this article.

_____

_____

_____

_____

Name _____ Date _____

Starting Small

How do the various parts of this piece unify your grasp of the topic?

1   The Spanish verb *tapar* means "to cover." Food
2 historians believe that this word provided the source for
3 the name of a kind of finger food—and a manner of
4 eating—that began in Spain centuries ago.
5   Back then, Spanish workers might eat breakfast and
6 then work long hours in the fields or at a trade. Perhaps
7 the first tapas were pick-me-up snacks to provide energy to
8 help workers keep going until lunch. Folklore claims that a
9 Spanish king ordered his people to eat small bites of food
10 whenever they had wine. This sounds like a sensible and
11 healthy idea, but is probably untrue. Whatever their origins, tapas are now
12 synonymous with a relaxed, festive, sociable Spanish style of dining.
13   Tapas are bite-sized snacks served between meals with something to drink.
14 Tapas do not demand particular ingredients. However, they do represent a
15 way to eat. The key feature of tapas is that they are small. Early tapas were
16 made with simple local ingredients. Examples include nuts, olives, eggs, or
17 thin slices of bread, ham, or cheese. Some areas of Spain also developed hot
18 tapas, such as fried fish or grilled meats and vegetables.
19   Perhaps you've enjoyed your own version of "little lids." How many
20 ingredients can you identify among these tapas?

> Every fall, Spain holds a national tapas contest. Chefs from all over Spain prepare their finest tapas in hopes of winning the title "Best in Spain."

Similar Concept, Different Cultures	
Argentina	*picada*
China	*dim sum*
India	*thali*
Italy	*cicchetti*
Japan	*izakaya*
Korea	*anju*
Russia	*zakuski*

25 Complex Text Passages to Meet the Common Core: Literature and Informational Texts, Grade 5 © 2014 by Scholastic Teaching Resources

Name _____ Date _____

Starting Small

▶ **Answer each question. Give evidence from the essay.**

1 In this essay, "little lids" (line 19) refers to _____.

○ A. covers   ○ B. fingers   ○ C. tapas   ○ D. ingredients

What evidence in the text helped you answer? _____

_____

_____

2 *Thali* are tapas-style snacks from which country?

○ A. India   ○ B. Italy   ○ C. Korea   ○ D. Thailand

What evidence in the text helped you answer? _____

_____

_____

3 How would you describe the manner of eating associated with tapas? _____

_____

_____

_____

4 What features do all tapas have in common? _____

_____

_____

_____

5 Suppose a tapas chef were asked to serve pizza with toppings. How might the chef handle this request?

_____

_____

_____

_____

Name _____ Date _____

Seeds for the Future

How does the article argue for the importance of seed banks?

1   **Seed Banks**   Living creatures rely on plants not only for food,
2   but for the very air we breathe and the clean water we drink.
3   In a laboratory in England, about an hour from London, an
4   ambitious project in botany* is underway. It is happening at
5   the Millennium Seed Bank (MSB). This is a state-of-the-art
6   facility for collecting, studying, and preserving seeds from
7   plants all over the world. It boasts large underground cold
8   rooms. In them, scientists have been accumulating hundreds of
9   thousands of botanical species.

> * **botany**
> branch of
> science that
> deals with
> plants and
> plant life

10   **Which Seeds...**   The botanists at MSB target plants most at risk from
11   climate change and from habitat destruction. They collaborate with
12   botanical gardens and other seed banks across 80 countries in this effort.
13   MSB strives to acquire plants before they become extinct. They provide
14   optimum circumstances to safeguard the seeds for centuries to come.
15   This will ensure their survival into the future. Botanists believe that with
16   endangered seeds safely stored, they can regenerate them as needed.

17   **...and Why**   Scientific understanding always moves forward. Because the
18   botanists at MSB protect saved seeds, they can one day sprout plants to use
19   in as-yet undiscovered applications. For example, medical advances might
20   suggest new plant-based uses against diseases or life-threatening conditions.
21   Or botanists might regenerate drought-resistant plants that could be
22   supplied to regions where water becomes scarce.

23   **Challenging Goal**   The stated goal of
24   the Millennium Seed Bank is to collect
25   25 percent of the world's plant species by
26   2020. So they are gathering seeds from
27   Kentucky to Kyrgyzstan. MSB currently
28   has more than two billion seeds in
29   storage. But with close to 100,000 other
30   plant species facing extinction, the
31   mission is a race against time.

Botanist at MSB sorting seed samples

Name _____ Date _____

Seeds for the Future

▶ **Answer each question. Give evidence from the article.**

1 How do botanists at MSB decide which kinds of seeds to collect first?

○ A. They begin with seeds from plants that grow farthest from London.

○ B. They seek seeds from plants that grow where there is limited water.

○ C. They race to collect seeds from plants that are nearest to dying out.

○ D. They look first for seeds from plants that grow best in cold climates.

What evidence in the text helped you answer? _____

_____

_____

2 Which of these habitats provides *optimum* (line 14) conditions for cacti?

○ A. alpine meadow   ○ B. grassland   ○ C. salt marsh   ○ D. desert

What evidence in the text helped you answer? _____

_____

_____

3 What does it mean to describe a facility as *state-of-the-art* (line 5)? _____

_____

_____

4 How does the photo clarify your understanding of seed bank chambers? _____

_____

_____

5 Based on the author's views, what problems might come to pass without the work of seed banks like MSB and its partners?

_____

_____

_____

Literature Passages

Passage 1: Troubled Times

1. C; Sample answer: I read each choice, and then reread the paragraph with that sentence. Will had serious news to spread about the safety of the Rutland residents (lines 19–22). **2.** B; Sample answer: I could tell by the context that the general was part of the invading British army (lines 6–9, 19–21, 38–39). **3.** Sample answer: Ellie is the mother of the McCrea family, and Daniel's wife. I figured this out because Will Dunn addresses her by name and tells her to take the children to safety (lines 3–5, 17–21). **4.** Sample answer: The story opens by describing relentless rain (line 1), which could cause floods and knock down bridges. **5.** Sample answer: The writer uses words like *dismal* (line 2), *worried* (line 4), and *times were hard* (line 6). The writer describes tension between neighbors (lines 9–11) and soldiers on the move (lines 6–9). The dramatic sounds add tension, as does contrast between quiet and noise (lines 12–17). Near the end, when the trap door opens, I thought it might be an enemy (lines 29–32).

Passage 2: Odysseus and Polyphemus

1. D; Sample answer: I read the "tinkling bells at dusk announced the returning shepherd and his flock" (lines 5–6). **2.** A; Sample answer: The soldiers were stunned at seeing two of their companions eaten alive, and figured the same fate awaited them (lines 13–16). **3.** Sample answer: A Cyclops is a cruel giant that has only one eye in the middle of its forehead (illustration and lines 6–7). **4.** Sample answer: Odysseus was trying to butter up Polyphemus so he would be more relaxed and willing to eat, drink, and fall asleep (lines 22–27). **5.** Sample answer: Using the name Nobody kept the other Cyclops neighbors from believing that Polyphemus was truly in danger (lines 28–29, 35–39).

Passage 3: Belling the Cat

1. C; Sample answer: In the story, *feline* refers to the enemy, which is a cat. The only animal on the list that is a kind of cat is the leopard (lines 1–2, 5–8). **2.** B; Sample answer: The young mouse's idea sounded great until a wiser mouse pointed out how dangerous it would be to put into action (lines 20–27). **3.** Sample answer: The cat approaches so quietly and sneakily that the mice have no time to escape (lines 12–14). **4.** Sample answer: A cat wearing a bell would make life safer for the mice, but it could be deadly for any mouse to attempt to put a bell on a cat. **5.** Sample answer: The mice realized that they had cheered too soon. The question made them see how impossible it would be to bell the cat, so they were still in danger (lines 20–25).

Passage 4: Charlie's Party

1. B; Sample answer: I read that Jumani made up the whole birthday thing as a joke, so Charlie was surprised and puzzled because he knew it wasn't really his birthday (lines 10, 12–16, 23–27). **2.** A; Sample answer: I wasn't sure what *nettled* meant, so I read on to see that he went reluctantly, and was annoyed (lines 8–10). **3.** Sample answer: It took place in a middle school on a Friday afternoon after school let out (lines 2–3, 6–9). **4.** Sample answer: He and Luther were collaborators (lines 1–2), there were secret invitations (line 3) and tacky party favors (line 5), and Jumani brimmed with mischievous anticipation (line 5). **5.** Sample answer: Jumani was a bit embarrassed by the three angry responses, but he seemed ready to try another prank in the future—just not a fake birthday (lines 36–39).

Passage 5: Triumphant Goddess

1. C; Sample answer: In the first paragraph, I read that Mahisha believe he could never be defeated (lines 1–6). **2.** A; Sample answer: The last line of the piece summarizes the story by saying that good triumphed over evil. So although B, C, and D have some truth to them, the key lesson is that good won out. **3.** Sample answer: The gods teamed up to create an 8-armed goddess, and gave her weapons, transportation, and blessings for success. The most important part was that they made her a woman because they knew that no male could defeat Mahisha (lines 8–18). **4.** Sample answer: I know that *tri-* means 3 (as in *triangle* or *tricycle*). I think *dent* may be related to *tooth* (as in *dentist*). So I think a trident is a weapon that has three sharp points on it. **5.** Sample answer: Durga's response was insulting because Mahisha was not used to being denied anything. It was daring because Mahisha believed he was invincible (lines 1–6, 20–22).

Passage 6: Mismatched Friends

1. B; Sample answer: When I reread that paragraph, I understood that Mama Snail was trying to make Snail aware of danger (lines 5–8). **2.** D; Sample answer: I know that crabs have hard shells and sharp claws, but in this sentence, I think *crusty* refers to Crab's personality, which is ill-tempered and mean (lines 21–23). **3.** Sample answer: Snail had been warned by his mother that the beach was a dangerous place (lines 5–8). **4.** Sample answer: Crab seems only to care about himself. She-Gull, however, who may have been hungry, was wise, observant, sympathetic, and generous with her advice to Snail (lines 30–35). **5.** Sample answer: Snail seems to take his friendship with Crab seriously, but Crab rolls his eyes as if he doesn't care that much (lines 1–4).

Passage 7: The Talking Dog

1. D; Sample answer: I read each choice, and the most likely thing to be next to a couch is an end table (lines 8–10). **2.** A; Sample answer: I know the word *woe* means troubles, so I figured that a woebegone dog house would need fixing up (lines 1–4). **3.** Sample answer: She was intrigued by the idea of a talking dog for sale and wanted to learn more (lines 1–6). **4.** Sample answer: Like a tall tale, there are ridiculously unbelievable events that characters in the story accept without question (lines 12–29). **5.** Sample answer: The owner doesn't think it's unusual that the dog talks, but acts more annoyed that Max doesn't tell the truth (lines 33–37).

Passage 8: School on the Set

1. A; Sample answer: The title is "School on the Set," and a science lesson is about to begin, so I figured out that Luke is the teacher for Jed and Abigail (title and lines 1–13). **2.** D; Sample answer: I reread the first paragraph, where Jed complains about starting science. It says that Jed always tries to stall beginning lessons, so Luke is used to it (lines 1–5). **3.** Sample answer: I learned that Jed cares more about his acting career and how much he will be seen by his fans than he does about schoolwork (lines 6–12). **4.** Sample answer: I think it means that Abigail isn't making any sound, but everyone in the room clearly knows that there's something troubling or important on her mind (lines 16–29). **5.** Sample answer: I think that Luke and Jed recognized that Abigail was unable to change gears at that moment to focus on science. Yet the lesson Luke planned to teach was exactly about the concept of remaining as you are until a force causes a change (lines 25–40).

Passage 9: Dark and Stormy Night

1. C; Sample answer: The title tells me that the story is set on a dark and stormy night. *Calm* would be a good antonym for *turbulent*, and the closest choice to that is *serene*, so I picked C (lines 1–2). **2.** B; Sample answer: Their car broke down and it was dangerous to be out in the storm, so they decided to stay in the shack (lines 2–4, 9–10). **3.** Sample answer: It means that nobody had been in the shack for a long time; it was abandoned (lines 2–8, 28–31). **4.** Sample answer: I think she's there to be the link to the past, to reveal the sad story of the lost young sailor whose sad parents moved away (lines 25–34). **5.** Sample answer: It's a ghost story, but ghosts aren't real. There are unexplainable things, like green glowing skin (lines 15–16), a salty puddle but no footprints (lines 19–20), and the recollection of a sailor lost at sea (lines 31–34). It is set in 1923 (the past), and the weird events were probably passed down by word of mouth.

Informational Text Passages

Passage 10: Two Into One

1. C; Sample answer: I reread that paragraph. I saw that Alice appears in both books, and that *Through the Looking-Glass* came 6 years later (lines 17–24). **2.** A; Sample answer: The article tells me that linguists study all areas of language, so linguistics must be the name of that subject (sidebar). **3.** Sample answer: The first paragraph (lines 1–3) describes a portmanteau suitcase as having two distinct parts. This is exactly how a portmanteau word is formed (lines 4–7). **4.** Sample answer: I use emoticons all the time as little shortcuts to show how I feel. I think *emot* comes from the word *emotion* and *icon* from the pictures we call icons. **5.** Sample answer: *Chuckle*. The question tells me that the *ort* part of *chortle* comes from *snort*. So I thought of a word with *ch + le* that's about laughing. That's when I thought of *chuckle*, so I checked a thesaurus and it made sense. Chortle = chu<u>ckle</u> + sn<u>ort</u>. Two parts of chuckle wrap around part of snort, like a little portmanteau!

Passage 11: They Fought Like Cornered Buffalo

1. D; Sample answer: I reread the piece to look for mention of each of these jobs. The one I didn't find was hunting buffalo (lines 20–25). **2.** C; Sample answer: I know that the Arlington National Cemetery is a place for silence and respect to honor brave people who died, so I think the best choice is C. **3.** Sample answer: The Cheyenne were praising the bravery, strength, and fighting spirit of those soldiers (lines 14–18). **4.** Sample answer: The writer tells us that the Buffalo Soldiers were determined, proud, and ready to take on any task asked of them, no matter how hard or unpleasant (lines 7–9, 19–33). **5.** Answers will vary. Questions might address individual achievements or general treatment in the Army, relationships with other soldiers and local citizens, what they did after military service, what they learned, how serving as Buffalo Soldiers affected their lives, and so on.

Passage 12: "Just Like Her"

1. B; Sample answer: I reread the first paragraph and found that Michaela had originally been named Mabinty Bangura (lines 1–15). **2.** D; Sample answer: I reread the paragraph about Earliest Memories. I know that nutrition is the healthy stuff your body gets from the food you eat, so I picked D (lines 18–22). **3.** Sample answer: She had been dreaming of being a dancer for nearly her entire life, and refused to give up a lifelong dream. She believes that dance is part of who she is (lines 25–35). **4.** Sample answer: She might mean that she lived in a terrible orphanage and that she was in a bad place emotionally because she was sick, lonely, unhappy, and lacked opportunities (lines 25–31). **5.** Sample answer: I think they must be very generous, caring, dedicated, and supportive people to have adopted a sick child from another country. They changed Michaela's life in every way, and must have supported her interest in and passion for dance to enable her to get so far (lines 9–13, 24, 34–35).

Passage 13: Savvy Shopper

1. B; Sample answer: I read the nutrition label for the Original Spoonfuls until I found the row for carbohydrates (nutrition label on right). **2.** D; Sample answer: The whole point of this article is to read carefully to know what you're getting when you buy something (lines 3–9) and both nutrition labels). **3.** Sample answer: Both cereals are made from whole grain wheat and both have BHT (which is for freshness). But Sweet-n-Frostie Bites cereal also has sugar, brown rice syrup, and gelatin. It is probably sweeter (both nutrition labels). **4.** Sample answer: I think the Original Spoonfuls cereal is the better choice because it doesn't have any added sugar, according to the ingredients list (nutrition label on right). **5.** Sample answer: For one thing, one label (Sweet-n-Frostie Bites) provides more information than the other. But more

importantly, the serving sizes are not the same. The serving size of Original Spoonfuls is 1 cup at 49g, while Sweet-n-Frostie Bites gives a serving size as 21 biscuits at 54g.

Passage 14: Lumber Lingo

1. B; Sample answer: I reread the first paragraph, which talked about the region's rich forests, and described how lumber meant jobs (lines 1–5). **2.** A; Sample answer: I read how obsolete skidways were left to rot (lines 27–32). **3.** Sample answer: Lumberjacks first cut down the trees, and then buckers cut those felled trees into same-size logs (lines 10–12). **4.** Sample answer: This essay is about words and expressions that came from the logging industry. So, I think that *lingo* is a nickname for special language related to logging (lines 10–12, 14–17, 20–21, 25–26, 29–32). **5.** Sample answer: According to this essay, logging was hard and dangerous work that attracted strong, quick-witted, and brave workers. There may have been actual people who were so good at what they did that people made up tall tales about them (lines 6–9).

Passage 15: Thank an Author

1. C; Sample answer: I know that *routine* means by habit or on a repeating pattern. The word most opposite is *unscheduled* (lines 9–12). **2.** D; Sample answer: I reread the paragraph about Jack London's life. Each choice is true, but the one that best explains his ability to write about adventure is that he had adventures himself (lines 24–27). **3.** Sample answer: Tyler loves reading realistic stories with challenging and unexpected turns, and that explore big ideas like loyalty, survival, and overcoming hardships (lines 8–9, 30–32). **4.** Sample answer: I think it means that Tyler's mind was taken off the problems of an injury by the even greater problems Buck faced in his difficult life (lines 13–23). **5.** Sample answer: Tyler was entertained and moved by reading *Call of the Wild*, and maybe used the letter to express appreciation. It's like a writer's response essay with some details about Jack London, which tells me that Tyler did some research. Or maybe it was a school assignment, like a book report (lines 2–9, 33–35).

Passage 16: One-of-a-Kind Museum

1. C; Sample answer: A, B, and D are true for many museums. The author says that MoMath is the only museum for mathematics in the country (lines 5–6). **2.** B; Sample answer: I read about the interesting

25 Complex Text Passages to Meet the Common Core: Literature and Informational Texts, Grade 5 © 2014 by Scholastic Teaching Resources

activities the writer described, and they all sounded unusual and original (lines 9–15). **3.** Sample answer: The writer's children heard about the museum and pestered to know more about it (lines 5–7). **4.** Sample answer: The writer was very impressed with seeing so many cool exhibits and children so engaged and excited. The writer was so impressed that repeat trips will include the entire family (lines 10–16, 21–35). **5.** Sample answer: I think it means that if visitors think the museum is cool, they may gain a new appreciation for math, and may be inspired to explore even more. That would encourage Glen Whitney to keep coming up with new and cool ideas for the museum.

Passage 17: To Buckle Up or Not?

1. D; Sample answer: I chose D because it is the only choice that does not appear in the piece (lines 11–14). **2.** A; Sample answer: I wasn't sure what *compulsory* meant when I first read it, but after I finished the piece and looked back over it, I figured it out. It means the same as *mandatory* (lines 4–6, 31–32). **3.** Sample answer: The writer gives information from the National Highway Traffic Safety Administration that says that it's 40 times safer to ride in a school bus than in a car (lines 16–18). **4.** Sample answer: The writer puts some words in italics, uses bold-faced words to begin most paragraphs, and calls out short summaries along the side to reinforce ideas (lines 1, 9, 19, 22–23, 27, graphics). **5.** Sample answer: Three facts: 23 million children ride school buses every weekday (lines 2–3); seats have 4 inches of foam padding (lines 13–14); putting in seat belts takes up space (lines 23–25). Three opinions: Making seat belts compulsory is a tough sell (lines 5–6); cost issues must be considered (lines 19–20); adding seat belts would have minimal, if any, impact on safety (lines 21–23).

Passage 18: Calamity Jane

1. C; Sample answer: I reread the sentence that included *faculty* and tried substituting each choice. I was stuck between A and C, but I don't think it's really an ability to cause trouble, so I picked C (lines 27–33). **2.** C; Sample answer: I know that to *verify* means to prove that something is true. The writer says that even historians aren't sure what to believe (lines 10–14). **3.** Sample answer: Both her parents died by the time she was 15, and she had to raise all her siblings in a wild and rugged part of the country (lines 19–23). **4.** Sample answer: I think the writer wants to grab readers' attention, set the stage for talking more about Martha Jane, and hint at

possible exaggeration (lines 1–5). **5.** Sample answer: She was a woman who enjoyed adventure like the rough men of her day. She seemed fearless and willing to do anything needed to make her way in the world. Her photo shows a rugged outdoors woman rather than one who would wear dresses and live a calm, gentle life.

Passage 19: The Earliest Americans

1. D; Sample answer: The writer defines anthropology as the study of human beings. Even though anthropologists may do A, B, and C, I think that D is the best answer because it includes the other choices (line 9). **2.** D; Sample answer: I reread the paragraph that includes *subsequently*, and decided that this words means that it happened later (lines 20–26). **3.** Sample answer: I think a hypothesis is a theory or important question to examine (lines 27–31). **4.** Sample answer: The author informs us that people did make their way from Africa to Australia many years before that (lines 1–4). **5.** Sample answer: The discovery of artifacts even older than the Clovis points and much farther east in our continent led some other anthropologists to explore the possibility of different routes to America. Also, some artifacts discovered in America resembled similar ones found in Europe from earlier times (lines 12–31).

Passage 20: Art of Its Time

1. C; Sample answer: I read the Confrontation paragraph and recognized that the only choice that was true about both Waud and Gardner was C (lines 10–16). **2.** A; Sample answer: *Pristine* is used here to describe the wilderness, which is natural land where nobody lives and towns have not yet sprung up. So I think A is the best choice (lines 4–8). **3.** Sample answer: Seeing the horrors of war shocked them (lines 14–16). **4.** Sample answer: I know from weather forecasts that ominous skies look dark and scary, like when a storm is coming. The artist might have been thinking about the coming horrors brought by the war (lines 17–27). **5.** Sample answer: Artists wanted to capture nature's great beauty. But the troubled times worried them, and they expressed that worry in their paintings (lines 1–9, 17–27).

Passage 21: Unlikely Hackathon Champ

1. B; Sample answer: When I reread the first paragraph, I realized that the noise of the dogs made Victoria stop being able to do her work (lines 1–5). **2.** A; Sample answer: Even though Victoria's mother was a software engineer, the big break came when there was a contest for exactly the kind of app Victoria imagined (lines 17–22). **3.** Sample answer: Her dogs barked, and she recognized that noise can be a deterrent. She also saw her mother texting while driving, and knew that was a dangerous habit that had to be changed (lines 1–5). **4.** Sample answer: A hackathon is a contest for software designers to compete to create the best app. There are time limits and prizes. Victoria was an unusual champ because she was so young and not a programmer herself (lines 17–28). **5.** Sample answer: Victoria had the idea, and her mother introduced her to a programmer, who helped move the idea forward. A contest encouraged them to make it come together quickly, and Victoria's team won the prize, which let them keep improving Rode Dog.

Passage 22: Making a *Camera Obscura*

1. C; Sample answer: This piece is about a kind of camera, so *project* here means to make a picture appear on a screen (lines 3–5, 32–33, diagram). **2.** D; Sample answer: I read in Step 1 that this is what you should get after you cut the tube, and I know this from math class (line 16). **3.** Sample answer: I think it's because light enters the camera's "dark room" through a small hole. In this case, you really use a pin to make a tiny hole (lines 28, 30–33). **4.** Sample answer: I can tell by the picture at the top of the page that the image comes out upside down and, of course, much smaller (diagram). **5.** Sample answer: I liked the introduction because it grabbed my interest. I think it's important for directions to be numbered in the order you must do them. It also helps to have materials listed first so you can collect them before you start. The diagram at the top helps me visualize what I will see through the pinhole camera. I'd add more pictures and diagrams to help clarify each step.

Passage 23: Transforming Trash

1. B; Sample answer: *Los Reciclados* means "The Recycled Orchestra." The idea of an orchestra playing on instruments made from trash is really unique (lines 6–8). **2.** C; Sample answer: I think that *ingenuity* means using your cleverness to make the best of what you have at hand. Cola showed amazing ingenuity by making the instruments (lines 13–21). **3.** Sample answer: Favio had the idea of bringing music to the children of Cateura, and Cola had the skills to make instruments Favio needed for the children's use (lines 13–21). **4.** Sample answer: What some people threw away, Favio and Cola were able to turn into playable musical instruments.

What was junk to some people became sources of deep pride for others (photo, title, and lines 6–8, 18–26, 30–33). **5.** Answers will vary, but should include something like this: Favio Chavez is creative, compassionate, encouraging, bold, resourceful, caring, and spirited. He saw problems and tried his best to find solutions (lines 9–19, 22–26).

Passage 24: Starting Small

1. C; Sample answer: I read that *tapar* means to cover, so I figured that another way to describe tapas would be to call them "little lids" (lines 1 and 19). **2.** A; Sample answer: I looked at the box called Similar Concept, Different Cultures until I found *thali*, which are from India. **3.** Sample answer: Tapas are small snacks usually served with something to drink in sociable, relaxed, festive settings (lines 11–12). **4.** Sample answer: They are small bites usually made with local ingredients. They can be hot or cold (lines 13–18). **5.** Sample answer: The chef might begin by making a pizza using local cheeses and vegetables or meats, such as olives, peppers, or ham. The chef might cook the pizza and then cut it into bite-size servings, or might cook little disk-size pieces. The chef would make sure that each pizza tapa had some topping on it (lines 13, 15–17, 19–20).

Passage 25: Seeds for the Future

1. C; Sample answer: The writer says that MSB strives to collect seeds from all over the world, especially from plants before they go extinct (lines 5–7, 10–13). **2.** D; Sample answer: I used clues from the sentence in paragraph 2 to figure out that *optimum* means ideal or best (lines 10–16). **3.** Sample answer: I think it means that the facility has the most modern, up-to-date features and goes for the best of everything (lines 5–9). **4.** Sample answer: I see by the botanist's clothing that it's very cold. Seed storage compartments are like labeled drawers in a file cabinet, very organized. It looks like a modern science lab (photo, lines 7–8). **5.** Sample answer: The author argues that seed banks are a way to plan for our future. Without them, we might lose plants forever without a chance to benefit from them. We might lose ways to protect habitats and produce enough food and clean air and water to survive.

25 Complex Text Passages to Meet the Common Core: Literature and Informational Texts, Grade 5 © 2014 by Scholastic Teaching Resources